LOW WATER FISHING

Front cover: the author at St Ouen's Bay
Back cover: the author's three grandchildren

LOW WATER FISHING

~ An Islander's Pursuit ~

David Le Maistre

Illustrated by Jim Le Couteur

SEAFLOWER BOOKS

Published in 2011
and reprinted in 2011 by
Seaflower Books
11 Regents Place
Bradford on Avon
Wiltshire BA15 1ED

Origination by Seaflower Books
www.ex-librisbooks.co.uk

Typeset in 11/14 point Bookman Old Style

Printed in Britain by
CPI Group (UK) Ltd, Croydon, CR0 4YY

ISBN 978-1-906641-28-3

Both the author and illustrator were fortunate to have fathers who spent time introducing them to low water fishing and this book is respectfully dedicated to the memory of:

Raymond John Le Maistre 1905-1967
and
James Edmund John Ulstrup Le Couteur 1905-1971

Contents

Acknowledgements

There are a number of people who have helped me with this project. Whilst it is not practical to name them all individually I would like to mention a dozen or so. In alphabetical order I say thank you to Karen Aubert, Brian Blampied, Graeme Bree, Tom Marett, Max de La Haye, Vernon Le Brun, Stan Le Cornu, François Le Maistre, my brother John and my late brother Richard Le Maistre, Norman Le Maistre, Peter Luce, Peter Pinel, Roy Vautier, Geoff Vibert and to Roger Jones for publishing under his Seaflower Books imprint.

My Jersey French is rather rusty and I am indebted to Colin Ireson from L'Office de Jerriais at Highlands College for his assistance and for reminding me of words I once knew.

Finally both Jim and I must express thanks to our respective wives for their understanding and tolerance during the writing and illustrating of the book.

Preface

I lost contact with my school friend, Jim Le Couteur, when, in 1954, he left the island and went to art school in Southampton. On completion of his studies he stayed on in the UK, where he spent all his working life. He lives in retirement with his wife Mary just outside Winchester. Whilst I only occasionally met Jim over the next forty years we were both aware of what the other was doing as I still chatted to his mother every now and then. In the mid-1990s we again made regular contact; since I retired he has made numerous efforts to get me to write a few words about low water fishing, something we spent many happy hours doing together, along with his dog Rolf, more than fifty years ago.

I claim no specialist knowledge of the subject, but his insistence that I should, at the very least, record my personal recollections of what I fished for, where I fished and who I fished with, plus the occasional fishy tale, finally persuaded me to put pen to paper. That is, more accurately, to sort out the word processing function of a laptop computer.

David Le Maistre
Jersey, January, 2011

Introduction

From deposits found in the middens and waste pits of the Neolithic people who, five or six thousand years ago inhabited the plains, uplands and forests where the Channel Islands are now, it is known that shellfish formed part of their diet. How much Neolithic man and his predecessors depended upon food from the sea and the sea-shore, and which grouping was the first to discover that the 'bounty of the ocean' was an important, and major, source of food is uncertain. An examination of the debris left by these people tells us that early man gathered oysters, limpets and cockles, for they left a quantity of empty shells behind. Other items which have survived include sharpened flints for use with spears and fish hooks made from bone. Thus it would seem reasonable to assume that early man was able to catch fish which lived permanently in ponds, in rivers or in the sea, as well as gathering from the shore. There is also archaeological evidence, as recorded by Mark Patton in his book, *Jersey in Prehistory*, that our forebears hunted seal, although I would suggest that it is many years since a low water fisherman came home with a seal as part of his catch.

To these early inhabitants fishing was a means of gathering food and sustaining life and the catch would almost certainly have been shared with other members of the family or tribe. In theory every member of the family or tribal unit, whether they were man or woman, young or old, should have been capable of gathering from the sea-shore and there was greater potential when the tide was out. What dangers prehistoric man faced from predators and other wild animals and how far he would need to forage we can only guess at. It would certainly have been very different from the gentle stroll down towards Seymour Tower experienced today.

At some time during man's evolution certain members of the tribe, or the community, would have acquired knowledge and skills which made them more productive fishermen. When this might have happened is open to debate, but one must recall that in far distant lands, lands admittedly at a more advanced stage of civilization, specialist fishermen were casting nets into the Sea of Galilee well over two thousand years ago.

Once acquired, the knowledge and skills of where and how to maximise the catch would have been built upon as it passed from generation to generation. It is not intended to develop these notes into a history of low water fishing in Jersey, but to record the activity in the latter half of the twentieth century as recalled by family members, friends and acquaintances.

I have tried not to stray too far from the subject, however I have included a number of topics which will be familiar to most low water fishermen.

It is sometimes forgotten that well into the twentieth century poverty was still widespread in some parts of the Island, particularly in St Helier. The ability to go down to the rocks and supplement the family diet, for free, encouraged many islanders to participate in this type of fishing, although the long hours which men were obliged to work would have left the average town dweller with little time to go looking for crabs and other shellfish to supplement his diet or fill the larder. Unlike their country cousins, many of whom would have been employed within family units, town dwellers would have found it difficult to convince their employers that they needed time off work because there was a good fishing tide. Many farming families combined farming with a bit of fishing and as such had access to a boat. This, with the advantage of having all the necessary tools to hand to fish at low water, would have made it easier for a farm labourer to provide fish for his family, in comparison with his town-dwelling counterpart.

I am not suggesting that life on the land was a soft option. It must be remembered that, in the early part of the twentieth century, agricultural workers toiled very long hours and that, despite the introduction of compulsory education, schools would be very short of pupils at certain times of the year, not only in the country parishes, when even young children were required to work on the farm. In a centenary anniversary booklet published by First Tower School, an extract from the school's log book for the academic year 1908/09 notes that some children were away for up to eight weeks during the potato season.

As the century moved on, smaller families and a greater social awareness by the insular authorities, resulted in abject poverty being marginalized; far fewer households had a need to supplement their food stock in order to adequately feed the family. Consequently, low water fishing was no longer something done out of desperation, or necessity, but became more the recreational pursuit which it is today.

There was something of a revival after the German occupying forces arrived in July 1940. Knowledge acquired or passed down through the family was still fresh in people's minds. When, particularly after D-Day in June 1944, many islanders found it very difficult to obtain sufficient food to feed themselves and their families, there were always the rocks to scavenge. Understandably, the military authorities were not over enthusiastic at the thought of hundreds of islanders roaming the beaches, rocks and gullies around the coastline, especially near fortified areas, of which there were many. The civil authorities did achieve concessions, concessions which considerably alleviated the hunger of the local population, although there was competition from the Germans themselves, who by 1945 could be seen gathering buckets full of limpets to feed their troops.

Some stretches of coastline were permanently out of bounds but not all beaches were closed all of the time; in certain areas it was possible for civilians to get a pass which allowed them to go low water fishing. You were required to show your pass to an armed guard at the top of the slipway before being allowed onto the beach, or the rocks, and the guard wanted to see the pass again when you returned. My wife still has her father's original pass which allowed him to go to Elizabeth Castle to fish. Obviously he was not permitted to go through the castle itself, as this was a fortified military zone but, instead, he had to clamber over the rocks around the outside, and to be mindful of the time because not only had he to ensure that he was not cut off by the tide but also because the curfew still had to be kept.

I have always considered a couple of hours following the tide down, even if there is no worthwhile catch to bring home, to be well worth the effort. The unpolluted fresh air, coupled with the exercise of walking over sand and rocks is quite relaxing, and is something which would benefit many people living in twenty-first century Jersey. They might even enjoy the experience.

You never know who might be fishing alongside you

A few words of Jersey French

Some species have a variety of names:

CRABS

Guernsey *ouais* (m); *houais* (m) *chancre* (m); *poingclios* (m)

Green Crab *vèrte crab* (f)

Lady Crab *démouaîselle* (f); *crabe* (f); *grégeaise* (f); *grégeon* (m)

Spider Crab *pihangne* (f); *pihanne* (f)

Small Spider *hueûlîn* (used in St Ouën)

Cockle coque (f)

COCKLE *Coque* (f)

Common *chuchette* (f); *bobbe* (f)

CONGER *andgulle* (f); *congre* (f)

Conger (small) *filot* (m); *filerêsse* (f)

CRAYFISH *crabe à co* (f)

CUTTLEFISH *seiche* (f); *cônet* (m)

LIMPET *baîni* (m); *écaillard* (m) (if large)

LOBSTER *honmard* (m); *mouaithe* (f)

honmard dé prix (m) (if full size)

OCTOPUS *pieuvre* (f); *peurve* (f); *pièvre* (f); *peruve* (f)

ORMER *ormèr* (m)

PLAICE *pliaie* (f)

PRAWNS *grôsse chèrvette* (f)

RAZOR-FISH *manchot* (m); *brioche* (f); *râseux* (m); *chuchot* (m)

SAND EEL *lanchon* (m)

SHRIMP *chèrvette* (f)

SOLE *sole* (f)

TURBOT *turbot* (m)

WINKLE BLACK *néthe coque* (f); *nièr vlicot* (f)

WINKLE GREY *côlin* (m); *gris vlicot* (m)

Y'en a-ti?

1 EQUIPMENT and COST

Before considering anything that a low water fisherman might bring back from his trip down to the low water mark to put upon the family table, let us consider how much it might cost him. One thing is certain – it is not as expensive as playing golf.

Low water fishing is free. You do not need a permit from the Insular, or Parochial, authorities, there are no subscriptions, no fees; it is entirely without administrative costs. There is no need to count your pennies, you can up and go when the mood takes you.

For sure you will require some sort of footwear. As a boy I wore an old pair of plimsolls, nowadays known as trainers, which I had grown out of, with the toes cut away. One disadvantage was that they let in sand and grit, but on the plus side the sand and grit washed straight out again. The point being made here is that you need something on your feet, and that a worn out pair of old shoes is perfectly adequate. Green 'wellies', with yellow draw strings at the top, may look impressive but when they are full of water they do slow you down, so do thigh boots, and you can be certain that you will invariably go deeper into the water than you ever intended to.

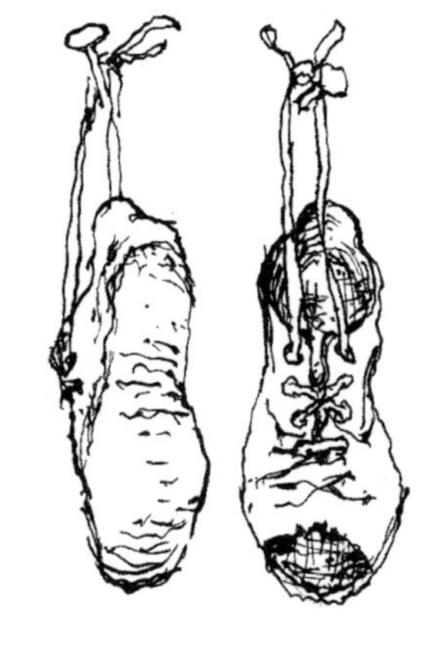

To prove the point I tell the tale of a Mr Le Brun, of

Val de la Mare, who usually went *au basse eau* in a three-piece suit, which was not an uncommon dress code amongst his peers. Not a Sunday best suit I hasten to add and no tie. Mr Le Brun was not a young man, but he was keen, and he liked to be first on the rock. In the early 1950s men would be waiting on the beach, carefully watching the receding tide before deciding on the most opportune time to make their move. On this occasion, with his cigarettes and matches safely tucked in the uppermost pocket of his waistcoat, Mr Le Brun set off to wade across to his target rock, but somehow he misjudged, either his route or the state of the beach, for instead of only getting wet up to his ribs, as was his usual custom, he ended up with water up to his arm pits and a packet of very soggy cigarettes. He was not a happy man that afternoon, his sole consolation being that, on other tides, many more had been soaked, and that many more would get equally wet in years to come.

So, all you need is an old pair of shoes, or boots, and some old clothes, loose enough to be able to move freely, sufficient to keep you warm in winter, with maybe a pair of shorts and a T-shirt for the summer. It is always advisable to wear a hat, for two reasons. One it makes it easier for your friends to see where you are, and secondly, it stops your head getting sun burnt in the summer. When you are down amongst the rocks you stand more than an above average chance of getting sunburnt, as people who have been down bare-backed will testify.

That's it. You are kitted out. You are ready to go and, with the exception of having to buy a new hat when yours blows away into deep water and replacing your sunglasses and mobile phone, which you will invariably forget to pick up after putting them down whilst you peer into a lobster hole, the approximate cost is nil.

Beware! Trouble approaching – from the east.

You will need some tools but here again there should be no great expense. For the crabs, the lobsters and the congers you will be catching (go on be positive!) you will need a hook or two. Except for spiking, hooks do not need to be barbed, as you will only be using them to coax your catch out of its hiding place, the congers will usually be gaffed, and the good news is that you can very easily make hooks yourself.

Go to a tackle shop and buy a size 10.0 hook, usually referred to as a 'conger hook', wire it onto a bamboo and you have a fishing hook. It is not difficult,

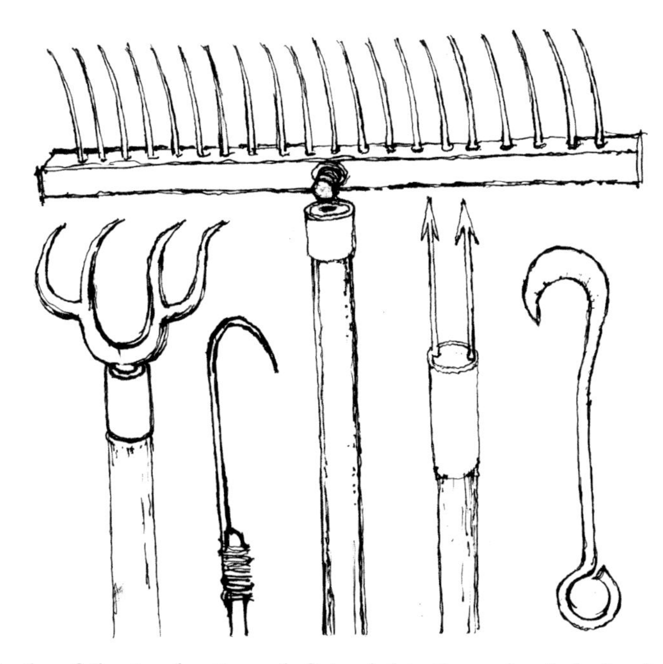

Tools of the trade. From left to right: Grappin; Lobster hook; Sandeel rake; Spike; Ormering hook

and whilst two hooks of varying lengths may impress your friends, it will not necessarily make you a better fisherman. A hook welded to a length of steel rod which is then attached to a stout broom handle makes a more professional looking piece of kit. Your hooks will enable you to catch a spider crab or two but, if you are seriously thinking of going after spider crabs a garden cultivator, or a hoe or, if you have access to one, a grappin, as once widely used in the cultivation of potatoes, is a better proposition than a simple hook.

An ormering hook is another useful tool to have. They too are easily made by any competent blacksmith. On my Uncle Hedley's farm he had a small forge, and he made all his own fishing tools, except barbed hooks.

To make an ormering hook he used a short length of one centimetre steel rod. It was heated up, bent over at the top into a hook shape and then beaten flat on an anvil. A ring on the other end, to which a brightly coloured piece of old rope was attached, made it a lot easier to find the hook if it was put down on the rocks or seaweed. An ormering hook is a valuable aid when trying to prise a Guernsey crab out of a crevice. If you cannot get an ormering hook made, you should be able to buy one in St Malo; that is where I got mine, but remember that you can collect ormers just as easily using a large screwdriver. Your screw driver will also lift off any limpets you might require for the kitchen, or the cat. Dr Frank Le Maistre claimed that the handle from an old zinc/galvanized bucket worked just as well and was easier to shape.

You can go spiking for flatfish with an ordinary garden fork, but a specially made spike makes it much easier to fish, and you are far less likely to put something nasty through your foot by mistake. All you need are a couple of straight-shanked barbed hooks; mine are twenty centimetres long (again from the tackle shop), a broom handle and either a couple of jubilee clips (which I have always called hose grips) or a short length of copper pipe roughly the size of your broom handle. Make a short groove down each side of the broom handle to bed in the hooks – this stops them sliding down the handle when you push it into the sand. Then either attach the hooks to the handle with the jubilee clips, or force the copper pipe over the end of the handle to firmly hold the hooks in place. It is as simple as that, and the second one is easier to make than the first. A fishing tackle shop at First Tower has readymade spikes but finding straight-shanked hooks in the island to make

D.I.Y.

your own spikes is now quite difficult.

For prawning you need a net and, as few people outside of the fishing industry have the ability to make or repair nets, you will probably have to go out and buy one. To collect cockles you will need a garden rake, which should be available to most people. This only leaves you having to sort out how to catch sandeels, and this will be discussed when we deal with sandeels in more detail.

Taking a sharp knife, even a comparatively small penknife, is always considered to be a good idea.

You will of course be catching something so you will need a suitable container to bring it home in. Fifty years ago it was not unknown for men to go home with a sack full of spider crabs, or half a dozen lobsters. Although those days are gone a sack or a basket is still useful to have with you. In recent years I have tucked a couple of supermarket plastic bags in my pocket before I go down and if I came home with one full bag I was more than satisfied.

From the above you will see that low water fishing is a very cost-effective pastime. A pastime which for minimal expense can put a veritable feast upon your table at most times of the year and which costs you, with the exception of a prawning net and possibly a sandeeling rake, little other than your time.

2 WHERE, WHAT and WHEN

Where to go?

This is a conundrum. Over many years, often handed down through families, fishermen have discovered holes, crevices, gullies, pools, etc. from which they have regularly collected, caught or extracted their catch. Not all holes are at first sight obvious and some are kept a closely guarded secret. If you know a 'special place' from which you have taken a lobster on twenty successive big tides, you are not going to tell the world and his dog where it is. So any beginner will only get general directions of where to look. If you regularly go to one small area of rock, you will very soon learn your way about and, once you discover a 'special place' you will always check it over first, provided the tide has gone out far enough. But remember that your 'special place' may be a 'special place' for others.

Unlike beginners, regular low water fishermen will seldom go down just looking for one species. They will check out a number of favourite spots and would certainly expect to go home with a varied bag. So be prepared to be confused. Following an 'expert' on a spider crabbing tide may not always prove to be the most productive way of getting a feed of 'spiders', for if he suspects that he is being followed your 'expert' will miss out some of his favourite stops and check them on his way back.

I recall an Uncle Hedley (I had two Uncle Hedleys) showing me a hole from which he invariably collected a lobster. As a bonus, there was a crevice alongside in which a Chancre, or Guernsey crab, could usually be found. The hole was deep, it needed a long hook, it sloped at an angle of about forty-five degrees and could only be reached on a very low tide. It is believed that many of these more obscure holes were discovered by farmers cutting and harvesting vraic, and some are still closely guarded secrets handed down within families. I have often wondered if my Uncle had found this hole in the first place or if he had inherited it like I did. It is a sad fact of life that as the older generation passes away all this knowledge is being lost.

An Uncle John (I also had two Uncle Johns) told me that an elderly fisherman, who felt that his low water days were nearly over, had shown him how to get to a group of rocks which at first sight it seemed impossible to reach. Knowledge and experience are important, and the more often you go down the more knowledgeable and experienced you become.

Although there is nothing to stop you roaming freely over the exposed rock – there are no boundaries or territorial rights. There is, or certainly there used to be, an understanding amongst regular low water men that they fished their own patch and did not stray into areas usually fished by others, unless of course it had not been visited for a number of days.

Some places are easier to get to than others. If you decide to fish along the north coast you are faced with small bays, some with difficult access, and a relatively small area to work in. There are advantages in this for you must always remember that there is only a limited amount of time on each tide and it follows that there is a limited amount of rock you can cover. By concentrating on a smallish area, whether it is a bay on the north coast or a group of rocks in the middle of St Ouen's Bay, you will become familiar with your surroundings and should quickly be able to distinguish features which tell you when it is safe to cross gullies to get to other rocks or reefs. The emergence of a head of rock, or of a stone becoming dry, or some other pointer will tell you that you can cross safely although you may be required to make a considerable detour to get there – and you may have to get a bit wet. Conversely when the rising tide reaches your marker you know it is time to return to safer ground.

If you go out towards Seymour Tower there is a very large and comparatively flat area exposed at low tide. It is a fairly long walk out, and if it comes on to rain and is blowing half a gale it is an uncomfortable trek on the way back. A heavy basket does compensate considerably for the discomfort. There is also the possibility of going 'off island' with trips to the Minquiers and the Ecréhous. Fishing excursions to the Minquiers are particularly

well supported when there is a good 'ormering tide'. Where you choose to go low water fishing is entirely up to you, but as a rule most low water fisherman stay fairly close to home. If you live at St Catherine you fish around St Catherine, if you live in St Ouen you fish around St Ouen. If you live in St Saviour you fish somewhere else, because St Saviour only has a couple of dozen metres of coastline.

Your choice of venue will depend on what you are hoping to catch. If you are after crabs or lobsters you need rocks. If you are looking for flatfish you need a clean sandy bottom. For cockles, and the like, a bit of muddy sand may not be a bad thing.

I am no geologist, but it is obvious that rocks formed by layers of silt and sand settling in long forgotten seas will present a far different type of terrain to the granite found on the north coast and St Brelade, and the conglomerate of St Martin. Different rock formations favour some species more than others, although most are present all around the island.

What might you catch?

As a rule the low water fisherman and the rod and line man will not catch the same things, they are looking to take different species. There are, of course, exceptions, the principal one being the conger. Although the majority of rod-caught conger will be 'wreck fished' from a boat, a significant number will be caught fishing with rod and line from the rocks around the island and still more will be taken at low water. The other group of fish we will be considering – that rod and line men also catch – are flat fish. Unless you have a boat and put down pots, the rest of the species discussed in this book are in the sole domain of the low water fisherman, although I have seen a spider crab brought up on a line at St Catherine's breakwater.

A few words of warning. You cannot go down and collect anything and everything, as there are certain restrictions on size. For instance there is a minimum size for a lobster, and some species have a closed season. There has recently been a total ban, now lifted, on the collection of ormers. These regulations are continually being updated and you are advised to make yourself familiar with current rules which cover both size and seasons before setting out. Full and abridged copies can be obtained from the States Greffe or from the Fisheries website. Do not fall foul of the law.

The arrival in the 1960s of affordable wet suits and associated breathing equipment resulted in an increase in people diving for pleasure and some divers took the opportunity to gather up excessive catches of shellfish which they sold. This was frowned upon by the authorities and a number of restrictions were put in place to police such activity. If you go down to the low water mark with the intention of diving – something

I do not consider to be low water fishing – you would be well advised to familiarise yourself with the current rules and regulations.

There are certain responsibilities which low water fishermen should be very aware of. You are advised not to go down on your own, although most have done it, at some time or other. You should make sure that someone knows where you are going, and at what time you expect to be back, which really is plain commonsense. If you turn a rock you are expected to return it to as near its original position as possible, thereby giving any marine life adhering to it a fair chance of survival. Remember that the underside of rocks which you expose is teeming with life, even if there is nothing there for you.

"You turn it, my back aches!"

When to go?

Low water fishing is a seasonal pastime. In May and June the spider crabs come up onto the rocks, they are available in the market a lot sooner but these are taken from deep water, in pots. Flatfish may be available from your fishmonger all the year round, but if you are looking to spike a few at low water you are best advised to go towards the end of the summer. Ormers are taken in the late autumn and winter. Winkles, they say, are best when there is an R in the month.

Whilst all of the above is relevant, the determining factor will always be the state of the tide. You cannot low water fish when the tide is in. There is, roughly speaking, a high or spring tide every couple of weeks. You don't have to be Einstein to work out that you only get two spring tides a month, but not all spring tides are as big as each other, so the occasions on which you can get down a really long way are few and far between. The good news is that it is not necessary to have huge tides to get onto the rock and that you can go down a few days before, and after, the spring tides. Going down after a really big tide is usually considered a waste of time because the rock will have been fairly well fished out, or at least it would have been fifty years ago.

The time of the low tide is about one hour later each day. Therefore low tide at noon on a Monday means that Tuesday's low tide will be at about one o'clock, and so on. These are approximate timings and should only be used as a guide. If you are unaware of the time of the previous days low tide this information will be of little use to you.

In the far off days of the fifties it was not unknown to go down low water fishing at night. In fact it might still happen today, but I would not recommend it. Spider

crabbing at night requires different skills. Adjusting to the surroundings is the key to success. There is little colour at night, even with a full moon. When underwater, spider crabs look white although they tend not to be so well hidden. Moonlight reflecting off the surface gives pools the appearance of solid patches of sand, so you get very wet when the nice flat piece of sand you tread on turns out to be an irregular shaped hole full of water. The only other night time fishing I have done is sandeeling – either raking for them at Gorey or netting in St Aubin's Bay. The sandeels for which we raked involved us strapping a two metre long pole to the cross bar of a bicycle and pedalling our way from St Helier, out to Gorey, with the sandeel box and rake on our backs. When netting I was just a net minder and no real effort was required on my part. I just stood there and did what I was told.

3 TIME and TIDE

Low water fishing is an 'at your own risk' pastime and it would be inexcusable not to point out some of the risks before going any further, even if a few appear somewhat fanciful. I say some of the risks because there is no accounting for the trouble people can get into if they try hard enough.

It is absolutely essential that you are aware of the state of the tide – by this I mean quite simply that you know the projected time of low water. You must be seriously thinking of moving back up the beach very soon after that time. If you can read them, there are signs which tell that the tide has turned. The gentle rise of the water will lift small grains of sand which float at the water's edge and in rock pools as they start to refill, and the natural line of seaweed will change direction as the tide starts to flow again. More experienced low water fishermen can leave it a bit later before they start to make their way up but it will always be your responsibility to ensure that you do not get cut off, and drown.

Following the tide down until the time of low water is reasonably safe. The Greenwich Mean Time of low water is published everyday in the local paper, so there is no reason for you not to know, but remember to add one hour after the clocks change in the Spring to British

Summer Time. Hoping that someone else will be on the rock to tell you when it is low water is not an acceptable alternative, so take a reliable watch with you. If you are fishing 'off island' be aware that the time of low water in Jersey is not the same as in the other Channel Islands and that the times of high and low water at the Minquiers and Ecréhous are also different to Jersey.

After the scheduled time of low water has passed it is foolish to assume that you are safe because you can see dry land behind you. This is not good practice, particularly at La Rocque. There are many treacherous gullies in this area where only a foot of water can be felt pressing upon your legs and where three feet of flowing water can sweep you off your feet. You must also be aware that gullies seemingly quite high up the beach can fill and become impassable, leaving you cut off and relying on someone noticing your plight and coming to your rescue.

There is a place of refuge at La Rocque, a cage on the top of a pole which is above the usual high water level which you might be able to reach, but this is an exception.

You must never forget that the further the tide goes out the faster it comes back in, so just be very careful and do not trust to luck. The incoming tide is not one-paced; it gathers speed as it rises. It is unstoppable and it comes in quickest in mid-cycle.

Weather does not present too many problems. Barometric pressure will affect how far the tide actually goes out. High pressure can push the tide out further than predicted, anything up to fifty centimetres, and low pressure, accompanied by strong winds, can hold it back by up to a full metre, but this does not materially affect the time of the low tide and should not cause a low water fisherman a problem. Weather-wise, if it is pouring with rain you will be uncomfortable; if it is freezing you will be uncomfortable. If the sun is beaming down out of a clear blue sky you will get sunburnt and be very uncomfortable unless you dress sensibly.

The main weather hazard is fog. It is very difficult to get any sense of direction from sound alone and if you are caught up in thick fog you have a serious problem. There is no simple solution other than to get safe as soon as you note the onset of fog. If you are inexperienced do not chance it and if you go down regularly you should know what to do. An experienced low water fisherman told me that when he goes out towards Seymour Tower he always takes a compass with him. Many years ago he took a compass bearing on his home slipway and feels confident that, should anything untoward occur, he will at least be heading for home in the right direction. Remember the incoming tide will continue to come in, it will not wait for the fog to lift.

There is a remote possibility that you may be struck by lightning. It is not unknown for fishermen to die as the direct result of a lightning strike. This is a very rare event but this risk should be borne in mind, particularly if a thunderstorm brews up whilst you are down on the rock with a metal fishing hook in your hand. In 1985 thousands of dead sandeels were washed up in and around the Channel Islands and an examination of those from around St Ouen's Bay concluded that a shoal had been in the immediate area of a lightning strike and had been electrocuted.

You will be repeatedly told never to go down on your own, although most have done so. Seaweed is very slippery stuff and a boulder, covered in weed, which looks like a solid piece of rock may move under your foot. It is good to have a companion on hand to help should an accident occur. I know from personal experience that accidents do happen, no matter how careful you think you are. In June 1998 I slipped and in landing heavily I ruptured the quadriceps tendon in my right knee. I hobbled up the beach to safety and, after a visit to the operating theatre, spent that night in hospital and the next two months sitting about with my leg in a splint waiting for things to mend. It took a further five months of physiotherapy before I was back to reasonable mobility. Be warned, rocks are a potentially dangerous environment.

You can, if you are unlucky, blow yourself up. There is still a quantity of unexploded ammunition left over from the German Occupation in and around the Island. If you come across a rusting, metallic, cylindrical looking object on the beach, or amongst the rocks, for your own safety just leave it alone. Report it, but leave it for the experts to dispose of. They will still thank you even if it is a false alarm.

Leaving aside the possibility of you inflicting damage upon yourself with a barbed hook, that is carelessness, you should never underestimate your catch. It is possible that it might strike back. It seems inconceivable that people would not realise that things with claws know how to use them. So be warned that little crabs nip, bigger crabs pinch, lobsters grip and chancres crush. If this is not bad enough, congers bite and, although with far less power, so do some worms.

Although it is unlikely that you would be looking for them, there are comparatively small fish out there which can sting painfully, so be wary of them. The Portuguese Man o' War, which resembles a jellyfish, also has a nasty sting and if you come across a stranded electric eel, as does occasionally happen, leave it alone unless you want curly hair.

And finally I make no apology for repeating my personal safety tip. Always wear a hat of some sort. If you are in amongst the rocks and your companions want to know where you are, a distinctive piece of headgear will be the first thing they will notice. Be safe not sorry.

Let's go fishing!

4 CEPHALOPODS

Not a lot in this category, only the now very rarely seen octopus, or cat o'nine tails, as we always knew it in the 1950s. They were then very common, and could be collected easily, and in large numbers. However the winter of 1962/1963 was particularly severe, when even the edges of the sea froze over, and the octopus went away, probably victims of the elements. Many were found frozen to death at the high water mark and very few were seen in the following years. There are reports that they are making a comeback along the French coast and are occasionally found in crab pots, but have not yet re-established themselves, in numbers, in the Channel Islands. It should be noted that this was not the first time that they had disappeared from local waters.

Although squid and/or cuttlefish are present in local waters they are not taken from the rocks. However they get a brief mention because, not only are 'cuttlefish bones' thrown up onto the beaches, they can also be picked up amongst the rocks, and man has found more than one use for them. Nowadays they are often poked between the bars of a budgerigar's cage, and they do make good pot scourers. During the German Occupation, when everything was in short supply, a further use was found for them. When grated down, they formed the base of an acceptable substitute toothpaste. My wife recalls using it regularly, prior to the Liberation in May 1945. Detailed instructions of how to make cuttlefish toothpaste can be found in Doctor John Lewis' book, *A Doctor's Occupation*, about his work and experiences during the Occupation years.

Octopus
The Cat o'Nine Tails

Everyone knows what an octopus looks like. They appear in horror stories, and horror movies, and have a reputation for being man-eating monsters, capable of overwhelming ships on the high seas. However they were not all as big as the giant monsters of fiction. In the 1950s there were a lot of them about but those I recall seeing amongst the rocks and in the crevices of harbour walls and the like would rarely measure more than a metre from tentacle tip to tentacle tip, although some were quite a bit bigger.

In his autobiography, *Footprints on a Winding Road*, Major A.F.A. Stamberg recalls a fishing trip to the Ecréhous when, as an eight year-old, he became entangled with a large octopus which required parental assistance to free him. Joseph Sinel, a noted local marine biologist, who in 1906 wrote *An Outline of the Natural History of Our Shores*, notes the average spread of an adult octopus to be about eight feet, or two and a half metres.

Although their common name of Cat o'Nine Tails suggests otherwise, octopus only have eight tentacles, all lined with two rows of sucker pads. The dome of the body is smooth, with two yellow eyes, a couple of propulsion jets, and a parrot-like beak underneath. Octopus have the ability to change colour as they move about. I always enjoyed watching a 'cat' moving about in shallow water. It was fascinating to see the various sections of its body changing colour and blending with the surface it was passing over.

The spaces between the granite blocks used in the construction of the breakwater at Elizabeth Castle were home to a considerable number of 'cats', as were many other harbour walls. When hiding under stones, or in holes in the rocks, octopus often gave their position away by untidy housekeeping. The area around the entrance to their lair was commonly strewn with the discarded remnants of small crabs and other crustaceans, their prey.

To actually collect octopus was not difficult it just required you to keep your nerve. The brave low water fisherman collected his catch by thrusting his arm into a suitable crevice between the stones of a man-made

wall, or under a rock which showed signs that an octopus was in residence, and waiting for the octopus to wrap its tentacles around his arm, or until he had a decent grip on the creature. He then simply pulled it out into the open. If a hook was used the chances were that you would tear the flesh and your catch would be damaged. It was an interesting sensation to feel the sucker pads move along, and around, your arm. Once out in the open the octopus was quickly dispatched by inserting two fingers into the propulsion vents and turning its hood inside out, effectively gutting it. As boys we invariably threw them away and left it to the gulls, or whatever, to dispose of the evidence, but it was occasionally acceptable to take a 'cat' up the beach to chase girls with. They duly screamed and scattered in all directions, all good harmless fun, or as it was more usually known, 'a bit of skite'.

Catching an octopus was not a completely one-sided affair. Octopus have three lines of defence. They have a reasonable turn of speed – remember that they are jet-propelled – they have the ability to change colour, and they are also able to cloud the water by ejecting a black, ink-like fluid which makes it difficult to see through so, with a quick change of colour, they can make a rapid exit in the ensuing confusion.

As people who have been to the Mediterranean will be aware, octopus make good eating. The sight of sucker pads on a plate has been known to give some diners a bit of a problem, but if you concentrate on the taste, and not on the looks, octopus are quite tasty. It is the legs, or tentacles, which are eaten, the hood and the membranes between the tentacles are discarded. How they are prepared is a matter of choice. They may be casseroled, deep fried or grilled. If not required immediately, or if you have a surplus, you can easily dry them and store the legs until needed.

It is almost fifty years since the octopus departed our shoreline but there are still people around who regret their passing and who miss being able to collect and eat the occasional 'cat'. Hopefully they will return again in the not too distant future.

I can recall a public house which occasionally put out bowls of deep fried 'cat' on the bar counter, in much the same way that peanuts are put out today, but that was before the octopus disappeared during the winter of 1962/1963.

An acquaintance, a mature lady who spent a lot of her free time prawning, admitted one day that she liked to catch a 'cat' now and again. She told me that she used to hang them on her washing line until dry and then snap off the tentacles, which she kept in an airtight biscuit tin until required. She grilled them. I was in my very early twenties when I was told this story and, to my shame, I still have this image of a washing line alternating octopus and old fashioned bloomers hanging out to dry.

Giants of fact and fiction

In his epic novel, *Toilers of the Sea*, Victor Hugo describes a fight to the death between Gilliatt, the hero of his story, and a giant octopus. Hugo's graphic description of the octopus, or as he calls it 'The Devil Fish', contains all the prevailing prejudices and beliefs of the day, which leaves the reader in no doubt that octopus were creatures to be feared.

Hugo's tale was written whilst he was living in exile in Guernsey. Finished in 1866 it is the product of his imagination, but there are some well documented tales, from around the world, of real life encounters with giants of the deep. Far closer to home, a report in the local *Evening Post* dated 19th August, 1922, tells of a fisherman, Frank Duhamel, being attacked by a giant octopus, whilst fishing off Corbière. Two huge tentacles were reported to have come out of the sea. One wrapped itself around the mast and the other around

Mr Duhamel's leg. Mr Duhamel slashed at the tentacle holding his leg with his knife until he was free and a Mr Gerard, fishing in the vicinity, came to his aid. Between them they were able to dislodge the tentacle holding the mast. A Miss Le Blancq, who was on Mr Duhamel's boat, was of little assistance, as it was reported that she was so shocked by the 'fearful sight' that she fainted. This story did not appear in Jersey's other daily paper, the *Morning News*, but it did get a mention in the *New York Times* on 21st August, 1922.

I had read about an incident with a giant sea creature at Corbière but was surprised to find this report as late as 1922 – my memory placed it in the 1890s and that a Mr Touzel had been involved. I have been unable to verify my recollected version of the event so I have to assume that I was mistaken, unless of course there has been more than one encounter with a giant sea creature off Corbière.

5 CRUSTACEANS

Which is the most sought after species of crustacean? For most people the lobster is the highlight of any seafood meal but many low water fishermen rate the spider crab very highly. Whilst it has always been easier to collect a dozen spider crabs than to collect a similar number of lobsters, it takes far less effort to obtain the meat from a lobster than it does from a spider crab.

From numerous references to spider crabs it is safe to assume that I am a spider crab fan, and although, at some time or other, I have taken home all the fish mentioned in this book, except a crayfish, praires and a turbot, I always enjoyed spider crabbing above all other forms of low water fishing.

It seems innocuous to include Prawns and Shrimps in the same grouping as crabs and lobsters, but this is where they have to go.

An indication of the importance which previous generations placed upon crabs and lobsters can be measured by the number of old Jersey families with lobster picks in their cutlery drawers, many of them in solid silver.

Chancre or Guernsey Crab

In Jersey this crab has a bit of an identity crisis. It is most commonly called either a Guernsey crab or a chancre, but English residents have been known to call it a brown crab, an edible crab, a flat crab, or a Cornish crab. Whatever you chose to call it is immaterial for they all look the same. It is a flattish, orange-brown crab, oval-shaped with a crinkled edging to the top of its shell – a bit like the edge of a pie crust – and a substantial pair of front claws which can hurt you. In the centre of their top shell these crabs have an indented pattern resembling a crown.

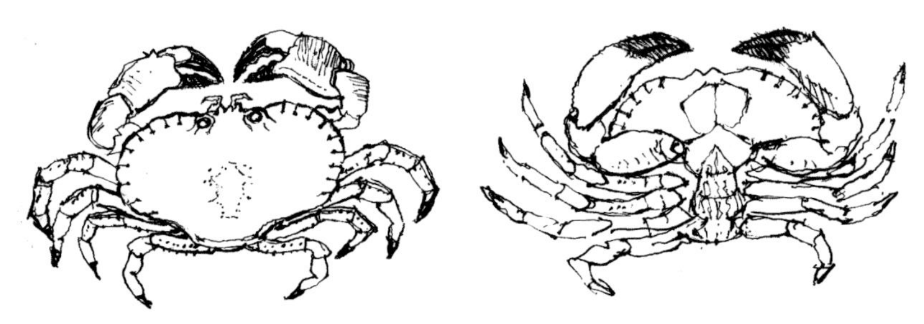

The male and female are very similar with the noticeable exception of an egg pouch which the female has on her underside. Big chancres live in deep water, but some do venture up onto the rocks, and being slimmer than the spider crab they have a tendency to secrete themselves in crevices rather than just trying to hide. You are not permitted to collect chancres which are less than fourteen centimetres across the back, but you can find them considerably larger than this.

Chancres are not fast movers and when exposed by the receding tide they wedge themselves in crevices and other nooks and crannies. It may sometimes take a considerable effort to prise them from their chosen hiding place. Having an ormering hook to hand is quite useful, otherwise an ordinary fishing hook should be sufficient to prise them out into the open and into your sack or fishing basket. There is no necessity for the hook to be barbed as you are not looking to impale your catch but merely to coax it into the open from where you can pick it up, all the while being careful not to snap off any of its legs. If, when picking it up, you hold it across the back, away from the claws, you should not come to any harm, but be careful not to let the crab squeeze your fingers between its shell and its claws – that hurts – and keep well away from its front claws, which have a powerful crushing grip.

Chancres can be found around most of Jersey's coastline, where the rock formations allow suitable hiding places, and as they have a much longer season than the spider crab they can be enjoyed for most of the year. You are unlikely to find anyone who will tell you the best places to fish for them, but just by being on the rock, and observing, it very soon becomes apparent where the most likely places are. Regular low water men rarely go down with the intention of just looking for crabs. They will certainly explore a number of holes and crevices and they would certainly expect to go home with a varied bag, so I shall repeat my previous caution: be prepared to be confused.

Having got your catch home you have to cook it – whether you should put crabs into boiling water, tepid water or cold water in order to cook them is not going to be discussed here. If your crab has been immersed in boiling water for twenty minutes – whether it started in boiling, warm or cold water – it is ready to eat. How you choose to eat it is entirely up to you, or your wife, or your mother, or whoever supervises mealtimes in your house. It is a matter of personal choice. Time past they would have been eaten at the table, straight from the shell, with bread and butter. Remember that we are not discussing how crabs are eaten in a restaurant or the dining room of an hotel, but how a low water fisherman and his family would go about eating the catch. After removing the top shell – by levering it off from the back – all you need do is remove the gills, often referred to as the 'dead mans fingers'. These are a varying grey colour and are not at all edible, one might go as far as saying they are poisonous. This applies to all crabs. Now you are off and can pick and enjoy your crab. It might be necessary to have a hammer and a pair of nutcrackers handy in order to get at the meat from the claws because these are very sturdily built, but the meat in the body is fairly easy to get out. Chancres are easier to pick than spider crabs – the meat is more compact.

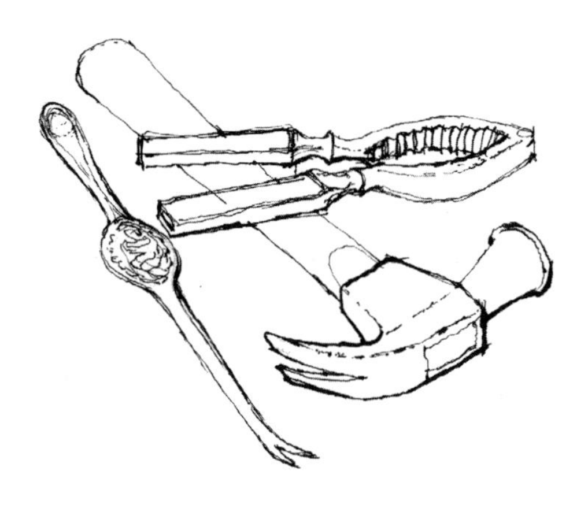

Spider Crab

Spider crabs are more rounded, or ball-shaped, than chancres and they have much longer spidery legs. They vary in colour from reddish-pink through to shades of brown, with marked differences between the male and the smaller female. The male has large front 'pincer' claws whereas those on the female are not much larger than her other legs. The female also has a very pronounced egg pouch on her underside, whilst the male does not. Males must be at least twelve centimetres across the back before they can be taken, although much larger specimens can be found. A number of other forms of marine life, notably Acorn barnacles and a variety of seaweeds, have made their homes on the backs of spider crabs and can be found attached to the top shell – an effective form of camouflage.

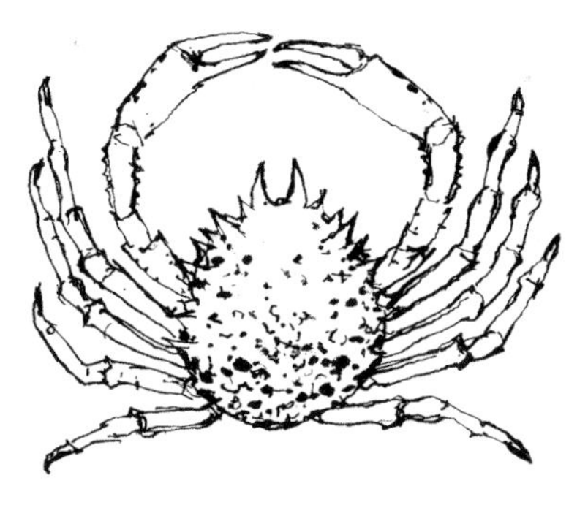

Almost all 'spiders' seen in the market or on fishmongers' slabs will have been caught in deep water pots which is outside the scope of this work, but for many low water fishermen the spider crabbing tides are the ones they await most eagerly. It is rewarding when lobsters, congers and the like are taken, but the spider crab can more or less be relied upon to be there in May and June and one goes down with every confidence of coming back with a feed.

In July and August, having made their appearance amongst the rocks around the coast, the spiders then migrate to the west until the water warms in the spring when they all march back again. Obviously there will always be strays and the exact timing will vary from year to year.

If you ask a low water man where to go looking for spider crabs he is very unlikely to tell you his own personal favourite place. However, spider crabs can be found around much of the Island where rocks exist, including the whole of St Ouen's Bay, from Corbière to L'Etacq, at Grève d'Azette through Green Island and around to La Rocque, and along most of the north coast, although some areas on the north coast are not easily accessible.

When looking for spider crabs, experience is a great asset. Knowing where to look, and what to look for, are skills learnt on the rock. No special tools are required – a hoe, a simple garden cultivator, or preferably an old fashioned potato 'grappin' is all that is necessary, plus a sack to put the catch in. As the rocks uncover with the falling tide, the majority of crabs will move away to deeper water, and if you position yourself in one of the gullies you can gather some of them up as they go by. Not all of them get off the rock and many, maybe by choice, remain hidden in rock pools or shelter behind strands of seaweed. The skill is in locating their hiding places and recognising the occasional stray claw which does not quite get tucked out of sight

It is not unknown for low water men to wade waist-deep along a gully, gently probing at the base of the rock with a foot, hoping to nudge a hiding crab out from the curtain of weed and into clear water. It is then a simple matter of lifting it out with a grappin or whatever. I have done so and it works.

Spider crabs have long legs which resemble a house spider's and they can move quite quickly. If you put one

Spider crabbing at night

down on a rock whilst you search for its companion, you are very likely to loose it unless you turn it onto its back. Once on its back it curls its legs inwards as if to protect its under side, and stays put – in much the same way as a hedgehog rolls itself into a ball. When rolled up like this they are much easier to put into a sack and most low water men will turn them over in their hand and wait for them to curl up before bagging them. Only the males have large claws, which are not really intimidating, and you are less likely to be nipped by a spider crab than a Guernsey crab or a Lobster.

For years these crabs have been neglected as a food source by people living in the UK, whereas in Jersey the spider crab is looked upon as a valuable addition to the table. In times past, the spider crabbing tides were something that people looked forward to. It was not unusual to see men wading chest-deep across to the rocks in order to be there first and so claim their piece of rock to fish. Nowadays, one can wait until the tide has receded far enough to stroll across without significantly getting one's feet wet, for there are seldom as many as half a dozen people fishing a group of rocks which in the 1950s would have had well over forty people on them.

Cooking spider crabs is simple. They are usually boiled for twenty minutes in a large pot – that's when they go a darker shade of red. In the days when they were more plentiful than now, it was not unknown to boil them in the 'copper', that large metal tub used for heating water on wash day. After sufficient boiling water had been drawn off to do the remainder of the wash, the copper was topped up with water and was used to boil sheets and linen. I have spoken to a number of other people who remember this part of wash day, but none of them can recall whether washing done after 'crab boiling days' had a distinctive smell.

As a family we ate our crabs straight from the shell, with bread and butter, and not too much else to clutter up the table. However, we have become far more fussy about how and what we eat, and it is now more likely that the crab will be pre-picked and presented as a crab salad, with many of the fiddly bits thrown away, rather than spend time picking the crab clean at the table. The shell is simply removed by lifting, from the back, which exposes the 'dead man's fingers'. These should be discarded but what else is discarded, or eaten, then becomes a matter of personal choice. Inside the shell of the female, one will often find a red berrylike substance, her 'eggs', and inside the male a brown substance.

Some people choose to discard these substances whilst others regard them as a delicacy, especially when spread on bread. The meat from the front claws of the male is easy to extract, and so to a certain extent is the meat from the remaining male legs and those of the female, although a hammer and a pair of nutcrackers will usually be required. The meat from the body has to be extracted from a number of individual 'cells' – rather time-consuming and perhaps one reason why these crabs are not looked upon favourably by those who have not eaten them.

At certain times of the year spider crabs have an unusual habit of massing in large numbers on the sea bed. Although the purpose of this gathering is unclear – some claiming that it is an occasion when they renew their shells and others that it is just a mating ritual, it does happen and mostly in deep water. A friend recalls an occasion during the German Occupation when one such gathering occurred in St Clement's Bay and, although the soldiers, who were bathing, would not let people into the water to collect crabs, they threw lots of them into the shallows for islanders to pick up and take away. As my friend put it 'there were a lot of full bellies that night'.

And finally a story about a bank employee, freshly arrived from the UK, who thought he would like to try one of the island's local delicacies, namely the spider crab. When asked if he had enjoyed his 'feed of spiders' he claimed not to have been impressed. Upon further questioning he admitted that having boiled the crabs, he had strained off the water in which they had been boiled, and served this liquid as a clear soup. The actual crabs he had thrown away.

Smaller crabs

There are only two other smaller crabs, excluding the tiny crabs collected for bait (see chapter 11) that have been regularly collected, sometimes for bait and sometime for the table, namely green crabs and lady crabs.

The green crab

Although called a green crab there is quite of lot of brown in the colouring of this crab and it is not difficult to find green crabs all around the island. If it feels threatened in any way this aggressive and snappy little crab, which is only eight to ten centimetres across the back, will rear up on its back legs, with its front claws spread wide, and will defend itself with vigour. There is very little meat in a green crab, other than in the claws, but they have been collected and eaten over many years, although I suspect that most will now be used as bait.

One does not have to go too far down onto the rocks to find green crabs. It is not unknown for them to turn up in children's fishing nets when they are probing about in rock pools. These crabs must always be treated with a degree of respect as they will happily grab a finger in their front claws and their grip is both painful and tenacious. The simplest way of getting free is to put your hand, or whatever other part

of your anatomy the crab has got hold of, back under water. The crab should then let go and try to hide. How Mum or Dad persuade their child who has put its hand into a pool and come out with a crab attached, to put the same hand back into the same pool a second time, just to make the crab go away, is a parental problem not a low water fishing problem!

The same principal works with most other sea creatures which grip you in their claws. Shaking your hand about might seem very proactive but you get a far quicker, and ultimately less painful, result by putting your assailant back into its own environment, where it has a chance of escaping the unwanted attention of someone who is trying to catch and eat it.

The Lady Crab

Similar in size to the green crab but whereas the green crab has a rounded shape to it the lady crab is quite an angular creature with red eyes. It has a squashed look about it and its claws and legs are also flattish rather than the rounded ones of green crabs. I have never liked lady crabs as a species, to my mind they have always looked evil. I have eaten green crabs but I have no recollection whatsoever of ever eating, or attempting to eat, a lady crab.

If any small species is going to survive it has to acquire survival techniques and the lady crab is willing to stand its ground and fight. If anything it is even more aggressive than the green crab.

In the early 1970s I spent a few months working in and around Aylesbury, in Buckinghamshire, and lived very near the village of Weston Turville which claimed to be further from the sea, in all directions, then any other village in the UK. Be that as it may, some twenty years later my former landlady, who had looked after me admirably, came to Jersey and we went for a meal. Because she was at the seaside she ordered a crab salad and there were shrieks of surprise and joy when her meal arrived for there on the top, purely for decorative purposes, was a green crab. This was a meal she never forgot, made all the more special by the addition of a humble little crab, which incidentally she did not try to eat.

Crayfish

Crayfish are a pinkish salmon colour and resemble lobsters, but without the big front claws They normally live in deep water and as such are very rarely seen on the rocks.

My Uncle Bert occasionally gave my mother a crayfish, which he said he had caught at Grève de Lecq. I had long had it in mind to ask him exactly where he caught them but left it too late. He had died and the question had not been asked. I have always thought that he caught them in pots. Not knowing anyone who could verify the source I was not going to include them in this little book until I learned that my Uncle John, whom I always called Uncle Jack (the same one who features on page 24) had collected one whilst low water fishing at L'Etacq. It was taken in exactly the same way as a lobster, and was cooked and eaten the same way too.

I have subsequently been told of a crayfish being taken from the rocks on which La Rocco Tower is built but I would venture to suggest that rock-caught crayfish are something of a rarity and that a low water man who goes down believing he will catch a crayfish is deluding himself.

But then low water fishing can be full of surprises and crayfish have been known to get tangled up in weed and unable to get away.

Lobster

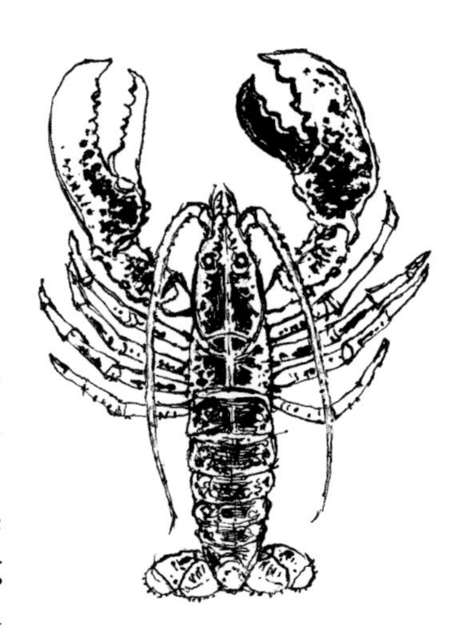

Live lobsters are blue! This might be very obvious to fishermen but it is surprising how many people find this simple statement difficult to believe. They turn reddish pink when cooked but whilst they are alive, and swimming, they are blue. Nearly everyone knows what a lobster looks like, two big claws in front, one somewhat bigger than the other, lots of little paddling legs underneath, a large head and a long body with a fan tail on the end.

Due in part to their reputation within the catering trade lobsters are not as plentiful as they once were and are increasingly difficult to find amongst the rocks uncovered by the receding tide. If they are there they will usually be found hiding in a hole, or in a crevice in the rock. An experienced low water man will usually fish a comparatively small area of rock and he will be aware of the best places to visit if he is after lobsters.

Not all low water fishermen go about catching their lobsters the same way. I have always waited for the hiding place to nearly dry out before attempting to collect my catch. If a hook is inserted into a lobster hole, the lobster will usually make a splashing sound with its tail and all you have to do is coax it out. Lobsters do not come particularly willingly and the entrance to many of the holes and hiding places will have irregular edges which, when covered in seaweed, give the lobster the opportunity to slip out unnoticed. If you have found a hole with a lobster in residence, or think you have found one with a lobster still at home, a few moments spent removing anything that might give your lobster a better chance of eluding you is time well spent, but remember that whilst you are doing this your potential meal might be leaving by another unguarded route.

I am assured, however, by a man who has far more experience of catching lobsters than I can ever hope to acquire, that the best tidal conditions in which to catch a lobster are when there are between twenty and fifty centimetres of water in front of the hole. With a little gentle probing, and a degree of patience, the lobster will come out facing the front thereby allowing the fisherman to pass his hand over the claws to grasp the lobster across its back. It is essential to get a firm grip because it requires just one flick of the lobster's tail and your potential meal will be gone. As a general rule lobsters do not return to the same hiding place on the next tide.

Lobsters will sometimes give away their hiding place by leaving the ends of their antennae showing. These should be easier to collect as you should be able to get your hook behind the lobster's tail and ease it out before it retreats into the far end of its hiding place.

In Chapter 7, which discusses congers, mention is made of the phenomenon of congers and lobsters sharing the same hole. You will not see a conger every time you catch a lobster but it is a possibility which all low water fishermen should have stored away in the back of their mind.

Lobsters can be found all around the coast where there are rocks with holes and crevices. All a lobster needs is somewhere to hide when the tide is out. If you are in the right place, it is possible to see lobsters swimming down gullies into deeper water with the receding tide. This is very much a bonus to any low waterman because, if the water is not too deep, he can stand in the gully and grasp the lobster by the middle of its back as it goes by and pop it, or them if he is really being lucky, into a suitable container and take his catch home.

Always be careful not to hold a lobster where it can reach your hand, or any other part of your anatomy if it comes to that, with a claw. If it does manage to get a piece of you, with either of the large claws, it will hurt, quite a lot. A supply of strong rubber bands is recommended as a couple popped over a claw renders a lobster a far less dangerous proposition, whether you take it from a hole or from open water. Whether this would have helped the lady who, in 1958, whilst fishing amongst the rocks surrounding Elizabeth Castle, caught a very large lobster is debatable. It weighed in at over twelve pounds (five and a half kilos) with a large claw measuring nine and a half inches long and five and a half inches wide [twenty five by fourteen centimetres]. Experts deemed it to be very old as it was covered in a variety of marine growths amongst which there were barnacles, sponges, anemones, zoophytes and seaweeds, indicating that it had not moulted for several years.

There are many ways of cooking and serving lobster but most will require that the lobster be boiled for about twenty minutes. In the immediate post-war years if lobster was on the menu of a low water fisherman it would have been boiled and eaten. It would not have been dressed or sauced or generally pampered, but would have been eaten for what it was – food. There are now so many ways of presenting lobster at the dinner table that it is possible to forget that fresh lobster, on its own, is a very pleasant eating experience.

In times past there were still fishermen working individually from various locations around the island and I was told about a man who fished St Clement's Bay. He made his own pots on the slipway at Le Dicq, and one of the hotels in the vicinity regularly bought lobsters from him because, at the time, it was cheaper to serve lobster to their guests than to serve chicken. This is not a low water story, merely a reflection on how times change!

Personally I am not a particular fan of lobster. The meat is far more compact than crab meat and in my opinion it is not as sweet. Perhaps I have not caught, or eaten, enough of them.

The last time I went fishing with my late brother Richard, an enthusiastic low water man, we went to St Ouen's Bay to do a bit of spiking (see chapter 7: the Flats). We were a bit early and the area we were aiming for was still covered by the tide. Rather than just wasting our time watching the tide go out we set to work with our hooks poking about amongst the rock which was accessible. In less than half an hour we had bagged five lobsters, two for me and three for Richard. We then went spiking and caught absolutely nothing at all.

There is a tale of a monster lobster having been taken in a pot off La Rocque, which I am reliably informed came about as the result of a certain low water fisherman who continually boasted about the quantity and size of the prawns he caught whenever he went fishing. His claims were totally untrue and in desperation a professional fisherman told him about a giant lobster he had caught which was so big it had to be broken up before it could be removed from the pot. This poor fellow, who did not have the wit to ask how the lobster had managed to get into the pot in the first place, now had a story to tell and he wasted no time in telling anyone who was prepared to listen about the huge, but unknown to him totally fictitious, lobster which had been landed at La Rocque.

Prawns and shrimps

It is difficult to conceive that anyone would not know what a prawn looks like. But, if there are readers who have not enjoyed that culinary delight known as a prawn cocktail, a prawn resembles a crayfish, or a lobster without its front claws, but considerably smaller. From head to tail, excluding whiskers, a six centimetre prawn would be considered a good catch. When alive and swimming about they are fairly colourless and somewhat transparent, but turn varying shades of pink when cooked.

To collect prawns you need a net which is pushed under seaweed and when withdrawn is, in theory, brimming with succulent, fat prawns. Obviously the more care you take not to disturb your quarry the more likely you are to net them. Technique is important.

Although not compulsory, many prawning nets have a flat front end which enables the fisherman to get close to the rock face and thereby maximise the catch. It follows that if the rock face is not flat a rounded net will be just as practicable. It is a matter of choice. Looking at old pictures of prawning expeditions from one hundred years ago one sees images of men carrying huge nets, and sometimes more than one of them, but a net with an opening of a couple of square feet will be all that you require. You will also need a suitable container to keep your catch safe until you get home.

Be aware that prawns are jumpy little things and given half a chance they will leap out of your net, or out of an open basket, which explains the very distinctive fishing basket which was formerly used in the Island. It has a lid with a small opening in the top to slot your catch through and is synonymous with prawning. No matter how much they jump the chances of a bagged prawn making it out through the slot is minimal. If you can not find a prawning basket do what I do and use a cloth coin bag from the bank.

The best known area for collecting prawns is outwards from La Rocque, in the direction of Seymour Tower. On big spring tides a vast area is exposed and there is little a novice can do by way of preparation. You just have to go down and try your luck. If you find somewhere which is productive make a note of it and aim to go there the next time you go prawning. There is no guarantee that you will ever find that particular spot again but, given time, landmarks will register and when you begin to recognise your surroundings you should be rewarded for all the hard work you put in. My brother Richard had memorised an area below Seymour Tower which he visited regularly, as and when the tide permitted, and seldom came home empty handed. The western end of the area which is uncovered on spring tides extends to the back of Green Island, another good prawning ground.

Fifty years ago there was a productive prawning pool at La Collette, near the new incinerator plant, but that has now disappeared under tons of land reclamation rubble.

Prawns need to be boiled for just a few minutes. They are small and cook through very quickly. What happens to them next is a matter of choice. At the risk of being repetitious, fifty years ago they would have either been eaten from the shell, with bread and butter, or pre picked and eaten with a salad. They would have been very unlikely to end up in a prawn cocktail, as the centre filling of an avocado pear or some such similar concoction.

Low water fishing trips to the offshore reefs – expeditions would probably be a more suitable description – were very much part of the social calendar during the first forty years of the last century. As well as photographs of these excursions, cine-film of family parties also exists. Nearer home, family prawning parties, often quite large with extended family joining in, would go down from various slipways in the late summer, sometimes finishing with a picnic on the beach. It is sad to reflect that today's hectic lifestyles leave little time for such leisurely and sociable family pursuits.

As boys we would sometimes go down to the New North Quay and, just below the cross wall, we would fish with a libby. This was a rectangular frame, with a net attached, which we lowered into the water. It was manoeuvred into position, flush with the harbour wall, and dragged back up, through the weed, trapping

assorted bits and pieces, including shrimps and occasional small crabs. I knew people who made their libbys with old bicycle wheels, and although it is hardly low water fishing it was a way of collecting prawns. Sixty years later I regret that I have no recollection whatsoever of what we did with our catch, if indeed there was ever anything worth keeping. I was reminded of our libby fishing days when, in the summer of 2008, I saw people using similar techniques fishing from Cromer pier, on the north coast of Norfolk, for 'Cromer crabs'.

Having allowed a story which has no claim to low water fishing into this chapter I feel able to recount the tale of 'Marmalade', who lived at La Rocque. Marmalade was a cat who frequently arrived home from his travels with a prawn, or small fish, in his mouth. He was a low water fishing cat who regularly wandered in and around the rock pools of La Rocque beach. On one notable occasion he returned home with a sandeel dangling from his mouth and at first sight it looked as if he had grown an oriental style moustache. Rumour had it that the sandeel had not been taken fairly but had been stolen from the house next door.

As a simple country cat Marmalade was never destined to become as famous as Felix, the Fort d'Auvergne Hotel's fishing cat which, in the 1920s and 1930s, featured on the hotel's postcards.

6 MOLLUSCS

The principal players in this category are Cockles, Limpets, Ormers, Praires, Razorfish and Winkles, and it is these that will be considered, although some might more correctly be classified as clams.

It may well be possible to gather other molluscs, such as mussels and oysters, as some must have escaped into the wild from the extensive beds now being farmed. However these, along with the whelk, are unlikely to be found in any great quantity. For the purpose of this work, they have not been included, neither have scallops, which are more usually dredged from the sea bed. I am told that scallops can be collected at low water in an area at the back of St Aubin's Fort. (As detailed a location as anyone can expect to receive from a low water fisherman determined to preserve his patch). I have never thought of them as part of a normal bag so I have chosen not to include them. My decision!

A word of warning. There are people who are naturally allergic to some of the species in this section and even if you do not fall into this grouping you are well advised to take care. Additionally, if a cockle or a mussel does not readily open when cooked it should be discarded. Contaminated shellfish can have quite a devastating effect upon your digestive system and you must always be on your guard, especially when eating out. If for any reason you think a mussel or an oyster or whatever does not look right just leave it to one side. Do not take a chance.

Cockle

No great skill is required to collect cockles, as they are not always properly concealed, often leaving tell tale signs of their whereabouts. A simple vegetable garden rake, not the sprung lawn version, is the most preferred tool. Cockles live just below the surface of the beach in areas which are regularly covered by the tide. They are equally happy in clean sand or sand which is a bit on the muddy side. By simply drawing the rake through the sand, where the cockles are, or where you think they should be, they are brought to the surface and all you have to do is gather them up and put them in a suitable container to take home. A wicker basket, which allows them to drain, rather than a bucket, is preferred but a cloth coin bag, from your bank, will do the job just as well.

Cockles should present no problems whatsoever, even to the most timid of low water fishermen. They do not bite, they do not sting, and they cannot run or swim away.

Cockles are no longer thought of as a serious, or major, food source. People nowadays think of cockling as something to do with the children. It was a good finish to the day to collect a few cockles and cook them over a driftwood fire before leaving the beach to go home. More seriously, cockles have been part of man's diet since prehistoric times. Cockle shells found in the middens left by Neolithic man as well as the rubbish pits left by our medieval ancestors indicate that they were an established food source.

Cockles are white to cream-coloured bivalves, with a ridged shell, which can grow to four or five centimetres across the back. The ridges on the shells can vary in colour, some being darker than others. They can be found along the south and east coasts of Jersey, where the sand is suitable, from St Aubin's Fort to the back of Gorey Harbour, and most places in between. They live just below the surface, and as they sit upright you can sometimes see an edge showing above the sand. I get a certain satisfaction when with a flick of my big toe I bring one to the surface.

Well washed in clean water and popped into a pot of boiling salted water it only takes a few minutes for the shells to open and they are ready to eat. If they do not readily spring open do not eat them because, as previously mentioned in the introduction to this section, just one contaminated cockle can make you very ill. It is, of course, possible to eat them without bothering to cook them. If you are prepared to take a chance, a knife forced into the cockle's hinge will break it apart and reveal the meat which can be swallowed whole. Not surprisingly raw cockle is slightly salty and is perhaps not to everyone's taste. It can be likened to eating, or swallowing, an oyster. Whether one should accompany such an alfresco meal with champagne, or with beer, is a matter of choice. I choose beer!

Cockles are often associated with the food stalls of popular seaside resorts, where they are served either fresh or pickled. Many day trippers will have taken home a jar of pickled cockles from Southend, or somewhere similar, and later wondered what possessed them to buy them in the first place.

Cockle shells have been extensively used in garden decoration (see Chapter 9) and also feature in that well known children's nursery rhyme, *Mary Mary Quite Contrary*.

Limpet

The first experience that my children had of low water fishing was gathering limpets. Having spent an afternoon on the beach there was the ritual of filling a small sandcastle building bucket with limpets which were taken home and boiled, before being fed to a very impatient cat.

Limpets are conical gastropods, which grow to a height of two or three centimetres. They have a large 'foot' with which they attach themselves very securely and firmly onto rocks, hence 'clinging as tight as a limpet'. In the early part of the last century, Joseph

Sinel, who founded and ran a biological station at Havre des Pas, known locally as The Aquarium, conducted a number of tests to determine the strength of a limpet's grip. His experiments revealed, quite astonishingly, that to remove a limpet, with a base of approximately one square inch, required a pull of seventy pounds of pressure. Larger limpets required greater force and, according to Mr Sinel, it made no difference if the surface was rough or smooth.

Limpets are easy to collect. They can be found almost anywhere along Jersey's coastline, but when collecting it is more usual to take those which are covered by weed, or in pools, rather than those which have been exposed to the sun for some hours. Be aware that if disturbed in any way, limpets will clamp themselves very firmly to the rock which they call home.

If you go down intending to get a feed of limpets it is advisable to have a flat-edged hook, or screwdriver, available to prise them from the rock. It is possible to remove them with a sharp blow from a stone, or large pebble, but this often results in a broken shell. Leaving an unprotected limpet in this condition is not something which genuine low water fishermen would ever contemplate.

Although few Jersey people eat them nowadays, they are still much sought after by many of the foreign nationals who have settled in the island. Limpets have formed part of man's diet for many centuries and as mentioned in the introduction to this book, limpet shells have been found in the rubbish pits which the Neolithic people have left in many parts of the island as well as in some of the dolmens. Empty shells have also been found in the waste pits of the Island's ancient castles. Whilst perhaps not the first choice that people would make when selecting a meal, limpets are edible and nutritious and were last commonly eaten in the mid-1940s when, towards the end of the German Occupation of the Island, food became very scarce.

In March 1945 the occupying forces launched a raid on Granville. Although the Germans failed to achieve their main objective this expedition, which rarely gets a mention in tales of the Occupation, was a partial success, with a number of German prisoners of war being released. The story is told that upon learning that they were going to be taken to Jersey, where the

"Limpets are very nutritious!"

garrison was surviving on meagre rations – some meals being made up almost entirely of limpets – many of the freed PoWs chose to evade their liberators and stay behind in captivity where conditions were far better.

It requires very little expertise to cook a limpet. Wash well, discard everything but the foot, put in a pan of salted water and boil for ten minutes. This timing is variable, but by then they should have detached themselves from their shells. Limpets can also be baked, stewed, fried or pickled and can be eaten hot or cold. They are, however, tough little fellows and the three recipes included in Lillie Morris' book *A Collection of Occupation Recipes* all require that the limpets be minced. Humble fare, but one which has served man well for many years.

Today most limpet shells are thrown away but they have on occasions been used for decorative purposes (see Chapter 9) and limpet shells have been used as a means of boosting the grit levels of domesticated fowl. Limpet shells, together with winkle shells, were

ground down and scattered in the poultry enclosures, or onto the fowl house floor, providing a cheap, and readily available, calcium based grit to help the hens lay eggs with good strong shells.

In the *Jersey Evening Post* of 6th August, 2007, there was an interesting little entry in their 'Twenty Five Years Ago' column, which stated that about ninety years previously, which would be the early 1880s, limpets were best collected 'in the spring before they had heard the cuckoo, as the old folk said'. I have absolutely no idea what this means, and neither has anyone else I have asked.

Ormer

Because of its uniqueness to the Channel Islands and the neighbouring coast of France, the Ormer has a special place in the hearts and minds of local low water fishermen. The outside of an ormer shell is a dull grey colour but the inside is lined with mother of pearl and is a very pretty thing indeed. Ormers are fairly slow moving and their shells have a series of holes along one edge, said by some to indicate their age. The ormer, which resembles the shape of the human ear, is known to the French as an *Oreille de Mer – 'ear of the sea'*. In recent years, they have become quite scarce in local waters and with a very limited season must be at least nine centimetres long before they can be taken.

Although much smaller than its potential relatives ormers are believed to be related to the larger Abalones found in South Africa and New Zealand.

During the ormering season, the larger spring tides will invariably bring out many occasional low water men eager to collect themselves a feed of ormers, but this can be quite hard work and on many occasions very cold work as well. I can recall being waist deep in the sea in the middle of St Ouen's Bay on a cold February

day and thinking nothing of it. Perhaps I am now older and wiser, or should that read 'less committed'. The ormer will most usually be found sheltering underneath a rock or boulder, although some secrete themselves in crevices in the rocks or in harbour walls. If you are able to turn the rock under which an ormer or two are sheltering it is a simple task to lever them off and pop them into a sack or whatever. If taken by surprise they will come away easily but if they are given a chance to attach themselves more firmly, a tool is required to prise them off. Either a specially made ormering hook, as previously described, or a stout screwdriver will do the job. If you are unable to turn the rock, or boulder, you can run your hand under the rock, or boulder, and when you think you have found one you pull it off, or resort to which ever tool you are carrying to loosen their grip. It is always possible, of course, that something else might be hiding under the rock but that is a chance you have to take.

St Catherine's Breakwater was a favoured spot to go ormering, as was the breakwater at Elizabeth Castle, although the generous catches of times past are now but a distant memory. Ormers can, or once could, be found all around the island. Personally, I am a dedicated St Ouen's Bay man, with only occasional excursions rummaging amongst the foundations of the breakwater at St Catherine's, and one memorable trip to The Minquiers.

When there is a big ormering tide it is not unusual for an armada of small boats to descend upon the Minquiers and to a lesser extent the Ecréhous, with resulting tales of exceptional catches, some grossly inflated – not an unfamiliar trait amongst fishermen.

I have been told by a reliable witness, and here I hasten to add that I have no personal experience of the event, that some years ago it was not unknown for parties of ormer fishermen who had visited one of the offshore reefs, to sort their catch very carefully on the way back and that all the small ormers, which the authorities might have considered to be undersized, were cooked and any evidence eaten long before the boat returned to dry land.

Although considered a culinary delight, ormers have a reputation for being tough. As such, once removed from their shells and having been well scrubbed, it has always been recommended that, before cooking, they are well beaten. I did hear of a lazy way to clean and

beat ormers which did surprise me. It involved a couple, from the north of the Island, who instead of spending time scrubbing their ormers clean, simply removed them from their shells and popped them into their top loading twin-tub washing machine. The ormers came out clean and the washing machine came to no harm. I told this tale to a senior member of the island's judiciary whose wife calmly said that this was the way she had cleaned ormers and confirmed that the twin-tub came to no harm.

The flesh of an ormer consists of a flat foot, with a protrusion, or crown, in the centre with which it connects itself to its shell. The area around this crown is where its workings are housed and here we have a bit of a problem. How much of the gubbins do you keep and how much do you throw away? In my family one organ, the *pitôsi* or *petôsi* (Doctor F. Le Maistre's *Dictionnaire Jersiais - Français* gives a number of other spelling options) was always regarded as a delicacy, whereas other families threw it away as waste. I have no idea why we kept it – perhaps it added something to the gravy. Personally I like *pitôsi* although I don't know what function it serves; it may well be a wise move to continue living in blissful ignorance of such unnecessary detail.

Ormers can be eaten fried, stewed or casseroled and with a rich gravy to go with mashed potatoes, are a genuine pleasure to sit down to. They also lend themselves to freezing as well as pickling and bottling so if you do strike lucky you no longer have to give any surplus away, but can keep them to cook and enjoy later.

The reaction of oysters to the invasion of grit particles has long been exploited by man, and it follows that an ormer, the inside of which has a mother of pearl lining, similar to that of an oyster, will react in much the same way and coat an invasive particle of grit with mother of pearl. I once had a small collection of tiny pearls collected from ormers, but regrettably this little treasure trove has long been mislaid, lost, or thrown away.

In their own right, ormer shells have a value and this is discussed in Chapter 9.

Praires

I have never fished for praires. In fact until 2010 I had no idea how easy they were to collect. I had always believed that they were dredged from below the normal low water mark. As such I was not going to include them on the grounds that they were outside my interpretation of what constitutes low water fishing. That was until, whilst casually chatting over coffee one Sunday morning after church, I was told that praires can be raked on some of the beaches off the south-east coast of Jersey, which admittedly is a long way from my usual low fishing grounds in St Ouen's Bay. My ignorance was total for not only did they not feature on my list of collectable species but until then I did not know anyone who had ever collected them.

Prairies are very similar to cockles but somewhat larger and they have a smoother shell. They are collected, cooked and eaten in the same way as cockles. A rake, a bag to put the catch in and knowing what you are looking for is all that is required.

When doing any sort of raking it is always good practice to concentrate on the area you are working as other species are sometimes brought to the surface. If you are quick enough you might well go home not only with a feed of praires but also with a few cockles, sandeels and/or razor-fish, and it is not unknown to disturb the occasional flat fish.

Razor-fish

A Razor-fish is called a Razor-fish because it resembles an old-fashioned cut throat razor. It is a bivalve, with a predominating grey-coloured shell, lighter on the inside, which grows to a length of fifteen centimetres or more. Discarded shells can be found on the beach, particularly just above the low water mark and the minimum size which fishermen are allowed to take is ten centimetres.

Razorfish live just below the surface of the sand, in an upright position, and leave a tell tale mark on the surface below which they are living consisting of two small holes resembling a key hole. Having identified the whereabouts of your razor-fish, there are two principle means of collecting, or catching, it. The first method involves the use of a length of wire which is bent over to make a hook and which is forced down through the opening which the razorfish leaves on the surface of the sand. A quick ninety degree twist of the wrist followed

by a straight pull upwards should bring the razorfish to the surface, whereupon it should be quickly bagged. The bend in the wire must be small enough to go down through the body of the razorfish, say one centimetre and must be pushed in far enough to go through to the bottom edge of the shell so that when twisted it will be over the outside of the shell and give the necessary purchase to pull it bodily out from the sand. This method obviously damages your catch.

The second method requires less skill and involves nothing more than a packet of salt. Having identified the spot where you think the razor-fish is, it is only necessary to put a small amount of salt in the telltale hole and watch for the razor-fish to pop out. It will come out quite fast and will not hang about for too long before disappearing back under the surface of the beach. There are no second chances because once it dawns on the razor-fish that it has been duped it will go back fast and quite deep. It does not tend to come up for a second look around. Be careful to keep your salt dry. Wet salt does not pour very well and taking a back up supply is always a wise move. A variation of the salt method involves mixing up a solution of very salty water, an empty washing-up liquid bottle makes an ideal container, and squirting the solution into the telltale hole of the razor-fish. Just as effective and it does eliminate the problems associated with damp salt.

Razorfish were once plentiful on the beach at Grève d'Azette, but in recent years there appears to have been a sharp decline in their numbers. Various theories have been put forward including the disturbances created by land reclamation at La Collette, but one thing is certain – it has not been caused by overfishing. Most that are taken today are used either for bait or for feeding the cat. They can also be collected in St Aubin's Bay, but I am told that the nearer you get to St Aubin's Fort the less edible they are. It appears that at the western end of the bay razor-fish are more likely to contain the remains of small crabs, presumably their food source and that you can sometimes detect traces of harbour mud in both the smell and taste of the razor-fish.

I was at something of a loss when it came to cooking razorfish because I have never done so and when I started to compile this book I did not know anyone to ask. My sole reference was Miss Morris' book, *A Collection of Occupation Recipes*, so it came as a pleasant surprise when an acquaintance told me that she still collects and serves them. I have subsequently heard of a number of other people who eat razor-fish regularly and I have been told that if you go to London you can buy them in Harrods where they sell for one pound each.

A friend who has lived in England for a number of years recalls collecting razor-fish for the dining table when he was a boy and that he was always very careful not to caste a shadow over his fishing site and that by keeping his movement to a minimum he increased his chances of success. He also recalled his Grandmother serving razor-fish and how much he looked forward to eating them. Yet another friend said that as a girl she often ate razor-fish and that they made good eating.

So much for my long held belief that razor-fish were only fed to the cat.

Winkle

Having suggested, just a few pages ago, that collecting limpets for the cat might have been most children's introduction to low water fishing, collecting winkles would almost certainly have been their first experience of gathering food to put on the dinner table. At just three years of age, my youngest granddaughter, Grace, was accompanying Papa, her other grandfather, on winkling expeditions. She collected for Grandpa (that's me) and, as was to be expected, her early efforts contained a few strays but she very quickly learnt what to collect and what to leave behind.

Although there are a multitude of winkle species to be found on the rocks surrounding Jersey, in a variety of shapes, sizes and colours, there are only two types that are commonly eaten – the smaller grey winkle, the *vlicot*, and the larger black winkle, the *coque* or *nièr vlicot*. It may well be that other species are collected and eaten, but certainly not by my family or acquaintances.

No great skill is required to collect winkles, you only have to go down with the tide and they are there, on rocks all around the Island. Unlike limpets, winkles have no means of gripping the rock, and therefore no tools are required to gather them, you just pick them off the rock, put them in a suitable bag, and take them home. Winkling is a great way to introduce children to exploring the rocks and as they can actively collect, either winkles to eat or pretty coloured shells, they go home with a sense of achievement.

If you are looking for *coques*, you would be well advised to go East. They are more plentiful at La Rocque than they are at L'Etacq, where they are comparatively scarce. Like limpets, it is best to collect from near the bottom of rocks, in pools, or under weed, rather than go for those that have been exposed to the sun for some hours. The variety you go for is a matter of choice. If you gather *vlicots* it takes a lot longer to get a feed, for the simple reason that they are smaller, but anyone from the L'Etacq end of St Ouen's Bay (my mother was a L'Etacq girl) will tell you that *vlicots* taste a lot nicer than the rather stronger flavoured *coques* from the East.

Should you chance upon a large winkle shell scurrying along, you would be well advised to leave it alone. Winkle shells make ideal starter homes for Hermit crabs, and if you accidentally take one home and cook it, you will see that Hermit crabs turn bright red in the process. Hermit crabs are not edible.

There are no fancy ways to cook winkles. After they have been washed thoroughly, they go in a saucepan of salted water and are boiled for twenty minutes. Personally I like to leave my winkles to mature for twenty-four hours before cooking as I believe this enhances the flavour. You cannot hang a winkle as you would do game, but the principle is the same.

How others choose to eat winkles is entirely a matter of choice. I know people who eat them cold and others who eat them hot, but whichever way you choose you have to pick them out of their shells. There are people who pick and eat, with bread and butter, as they go along, others will pick a feed and eat later. Owning a special 'winkle picking pin' helps. I bought my set of six in St Malo which are about seven centimetres long, each with a different coloured ball on one end. In our house there was never any dispute as to which one you used, we were colour coded. There is no waste on a winkle, once you have removed the protective shield, at the entrance to the shell, everything else is edible.

It is possible to pickle winkles but it is difficult to envisage that an old time Jerseyman would have gone to the trouble of pickling, when all he had to do was go down to the beach and collect a feed any time he wanted.

Winkle shells lend themselves to recycling and, like limpet shells, were an inexpensive source of grit in the fowl house. My personal recollections come from the occupation years. Once the winkles had been eaten the empty shells would be ground down and scattered, as a calcium-rich grit, onto the fowl house floor.

Empty winkle shells have also been used for decorative purpose (see Chapter 9).

Although I have visited all of the principal Channel Islands I have not, with one exception, tried my luck at low water fishing in the other islands. I do not feel comfortable with the idea of asking a hotel chef to cook my catch, should there be one. The exception was when we stayed in self-catering accommodation near Bordeaux Harbour in Guernsey. With the children's assistance some carefully selected winkles were gathered and brought back to the chalet destined for the pot that evening. We then went to visit friends who invited us to stay for a meal and as we were returning to Jersey the next day we never got around to eating our 'foreign' winkles. At about ten that evening I was dispatched to Bordeaux Harbour to put them back on the rocks from which they had been collected.

7 WET FISH

I have limited this chapter to the five fish which a low waterman might reasonably expect to catch at some time during his time down at the low water mark.

I had originally planned a chapter on eels, to include the conger and the sandeel, and it was not until I started writing about sandeels that I realized that sandeels are fish. They are not eels!

I had also intended a separate section on the three flat fish which it is possible to catch when spiking but they too are now included in this all inclusive section which I have entitled Wet Fish.

It was suggested to me, by a man who claimed to have found a mackerel stranded by the falling tide in a rock pool that I should include mackerel, and one other fish the name of which I can no longer recall. I am sure his suggestion was well meant but I have decided that this is outside the scope of this work.

Conger

Congers are grey/black eels which can grow up to three metres long (ten feet), with a girth of forty five to fifty centimetres (say one and a half feet). Those from the West of the island are darker than those from the East of the island – possibly a means of camouflage. Congers have a reputation for being quite dangerous and aggressive fish, fish which are very strong and have a powerful bite. Low water fishermen would not normally expect to find congers as big as those caught by rod and line 'wreck' fishermen but, nevertheless, large specimens have been taken from the rocks

Congers can be found all around the Island. At low water they will be secreted in holes, sometimes quite deep holes, and need to be manually hauled out with a hook, although they can sometimes be persuaded to do a lot of the work themselves by teasing them out of their hiding place. It requires a suitably strong basket, or sack, to secure the catch, remembering all the while that it is not clever to let any conger, however small, get its teeth into your fingers, hands, arms or ankles. They can also inflict damage from the other end and a thrash of a conger's tail can knock a man off his feet, especially if he is standing on slippery seaweed.

Should you disturb a conger and it manages to get away it is likely to return to the same hiding place and you can be fairly confident of having another chance to catch it the following day.

Although I have not personally experienced it I am told that even after being dead for some hours, a conger's jaw can snap shut and inflict a nasty wound, and to make matters worse it can still happen after the head and body have been separated. So never leave a dead conger's mouth open to show your friends its teeth, it could have embarrassing consequences.

If you have been lucky, or skilful, enough to have found a conger you should never forget the old fisherman's tale about the conger's best friend. For reasons unexplained it is not uncommon for a conger to share its hiding place – lair sounds far more appropriate for this fierce beast – with a lobster. The lobster will be nearest the entrance and will normally be positioned at an angle, enabling it to keep an eye on the conger.

The flesh of the conger has long been a feature of the locals' diet. In the Middle Ages the Channel Islands were involved in a flourishing trade in conger meat, which was dried and salted, and there are numerous, well documented accounts concerning the trade in conger. The importance of this trade to our forebears is borne out by the number of legal disputes concerning the rights of just about everyone from the King, the Church, the Seigneurs, the Fishermen *et al*, all well recorded in G.F.B. de Gruchy's book *Mediaeval Land Tenures in Jersey*.

It is not inconceivable that these preserving skills were still practised, on a far smaller scale, in ensuing centuries. Might they have played a part in the development of the Newfoundland cod fishing industry, a trade based on the drying and salting of fish and the export of the same which generated considerable wealth to certain sections of the island in the nineteenth century.

Nowadays if a conger comes home from a low water fishing trip it will invariably be cut into steaks and be fried or baked. Congers can be big fish and the refrigerator, and/or the deep freeze, have resolved the problem of how to save that portion of the catch which

might not be immediately required. The necessity to dry, or salt down, any surplus has been removed from the equation. A conger steak, fried in butter, is a memorable eating experience.

Prior to cooking a conger steak it is not unknown in some Jersey kitchens to place the steak between tea towels, with a weight on top, to remove some of the oil. It is claimed that this enhances the flavour, but it then requires additional butter to fry it up properly. Throw away absorbent kitchen towels are just as efficient as tea towels and save a lot of oily washing.

Conger also features on the menu in another well known local dish, conger soup, and there are probably as many recipes for conger soup as there are for making bean crocks and everyone will claim their recipe to be the original and the best. All of them require that bits of the conger, usually the head and tail, be boiled in milk, or milk and water, for as long as is thought desirable. Into this stock, when strained, may be added, according to the recipe you are following, various other ingredients, carrot being the most popular. You can, of course, reintroduce any pieces of conger meat which were filtered out during straining. Most recipes will suggest that a few marigolds petals be sprinkled on top of the soup when served.

Mention was made on page 24 about my Uncle Jack having been told of a way of getting to a certain group of rocks by an old fisherman, and it was from these rocks that his son, my cousin Norman, and some friends collected a huge haul of conger in February 1952. The largest weighed over 15 kilos and the catch was considered to be sufficiently noteworthy that it was featured in the *Jersey Evening Post*.

Sandeel

Depending on when, where and how, they are caught, sandeels come in various sizes, which is not totally surprising as there are two species which live in and around the gravel banks of Jersey. The Greater Sandeel, or Green Sandeel, is the larger of the two and averages about sixteen centimetres in length. There is also the smaller but more numerous Lesser or Red Sandeel. Sandeels are slender silvery fish (not eels) which shelter in sand banks and swim in shoals.

Sandeels can be collected in one of two ways, both of which fall within the remit of low water fishing. They can be caught either in nets or, more usually, can be raked from the sand banks in which they shelter or rest.

To collect with nets requires a number of people working as a team. Having located a shoal of sandeel it is directed in the general direction of the net, at this stage spread as wide as possible, and then gradually the circle of net is closed thereby trapping the shoal and taking home the spoils. I remember doing this at night in St Aubin's Bay many years ago, something which I now believe to be illegal. To catch sandeels in nets it is necessary to have a large area of sand and St Aubin's Bay, St Ouen's Bay and the Royal Bay of Grouville are obvious choices.

The more usual way to collect sandeels is to rake them from the sand banks in which they are hidden, and here again there are a number of ways of doing this. The most common form of rake is a long-handled rake with a fifty to sixty centimetre head which has sharp metal tines ten centimetres long. This is drawn through the surface of the sand where you think the sandeels may be, and if you are right they are impaled or stranded on the tines and you knock them off into your collecting box, which is the same length as the head of your rake and which is hung around your neck. You need to be fairly quick as sandeels do not take kindly to being disturbed and will wriggle furiously as they struggle to escape. This method can damage the catch, but it does not require any bending, as the head of the rake is brought level with the box and the catch dropped straight into it. Warning: Sandeeling boxes tend to be quite heavy, and so does the rake.

Sandeels can be raked up with an ordinary garden rake, not the sprung lawn type, but it is then necessary to collect them by hand. They are fairly swift moving creatures, and slippery with it, but you can be selective and little damage is done to the catch. You will inevitably do quite a lot of bending as you collect them. A friend told me that his chosen method was to use a wooden hay making rake, which, he claimed, did not damage the sandeel in any way. I was also told by one man that he just dug them out with an ordinary garden fork.

There is yet another implement which some low water fishermen prefer and this is a small sickle, a specialist piece of equipment once used for cutting seaweed from the rocks. This is a hands and knees job, but by running the sickle slowly through the sand the sandeel are brought to the surface, collected by hand and bagged. An article in an 1855 edition of *Chambers Magazine* has a very descriptive account of a sandeeling expedition where sickles were the preferred tool.

The best known area for sandeeling is the vast expanse of sand exposed in the direction of Seymour Tower, on the south-east corner of the island. If it is the right time of year and you have the necessary equipment all you need to do is take your chosen rake and go down to where everyone else is. It is not possible for the regulars to hide favourite fishing spots in the flat open stretches of sand. Where they go, you go. No great skill required here, but sandeel sometimes move from one area of sand or gravel to another without warning. You have to find them.

The French name for Plémont Bay implies that it should be a productive spot, it is *Grève au Lanchon*, or *Lançon*, in simple translation Sandeel Beach.

Before I was married I lived in the Royal Crescent, in St Helier, and my brothers and I saw nothing unusual in cycling out to Gorey, on a fine evening, with our sandeel boxes and rakes strapped to our bikes. The sandbanks just off the end of the pier were our goal and, with the pier head lights to help us see, it made no difference how dark it became. On 3rd March, 1965, there was a severe storm which washed away the end of the pier. During the course of rebuilding, heavy machinery was driven all over the sand banks which we had fished and I believe the sandeels went away. I have not tried to fish there since the pier head was rebuilt

When eaten fresh the larger sandeels would usually be gutted, sometimes leaving the heads on, and fried. They are a very tasty fish and make an excellent meal, more so when fried in butter. If not used for making chervie, tiny sandeels were fried in a pan and eaten whole, that is to say you ate the lot, from head to tail and everything in between.

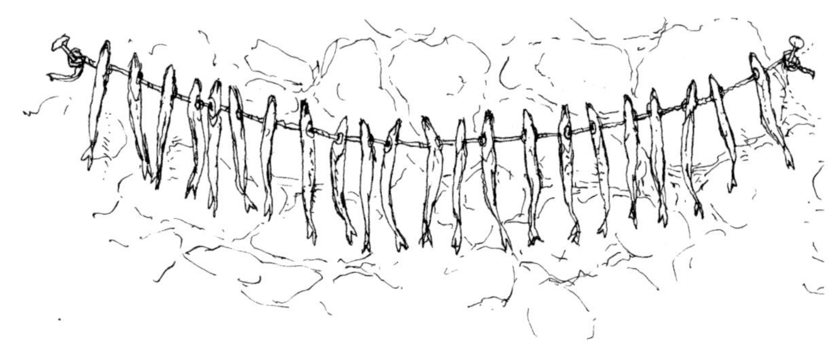

Sandeels are ideal for drying, they are not very thick and dry quickly. We were amateur low water fishermen who dried them by threading a length of string through their eye sockets and hanging them against the south facing back garden wall. Before our marriage my wife lived next door to a more dedicated low water man and he had made special metal trays, she believes out of meat safe wire gauze, on which he laid out his catch. With suitable hooked supports he was able to hang the trays from his wife's washing line.

Sandeels make very good bait for rod and line fishermen – see chapter 11. They freeze well and if an occasional fisherman decides to try his luck one evening a few frozen sandeels in the fridge come in useful. They are also extensively used by professional fishermen.

The Flats

How does a low water fisherman catch a flat fish? That is a question that has been asked more than once, and the simple answer is either by stabbing them through the back with a spike, or by trapping them in a net. Spiking was originally done with an ordinary pointed garden fork, like those used for digging potatoes, and although most fisherman now use a specially made spike, usually two, one in each hand – it is still possible to see the older fork method being used, with all the inherent danger of impaling your foot. Netting requires a team of helpers and is done in the same way as described in the chapter on Sandeels.

Whichever method you choose there are three possible fish which you might catch.

Plaice

The classic flat fish. Shaped like a rounded lozenge, with circular orange brown spot markings. It can be found in most of the island's sandy bays, and in sandy-bottomed rock pools, but more usually fished for at St Ouen's Bay and off La Rocque.

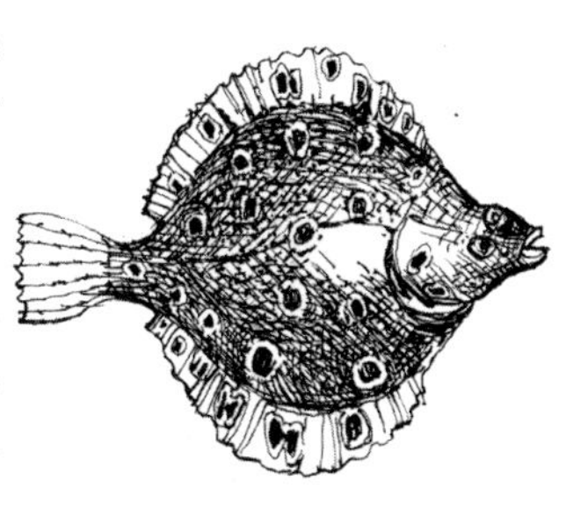

Sole

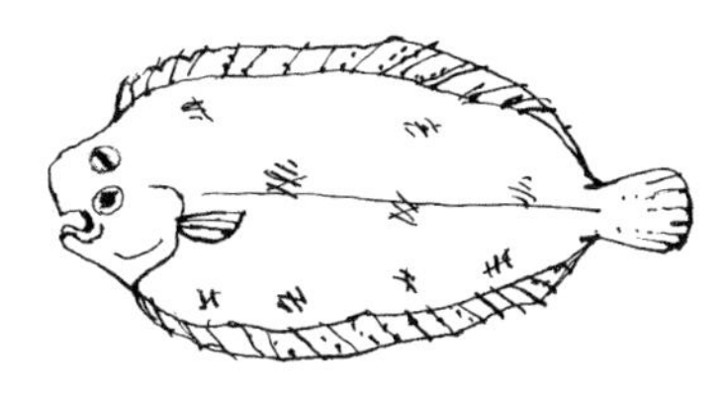

Grey in colour and more of a rectangular shape. They are regularly taken from St Ouen's Bay but rarely, if ever, seen anywhere else around the island.

Turbot

For all intents and purposes this fish is just a larger version of the plaice. They are known to have been caught in St Ouen's Bay, but are rarely seen anywhere else.

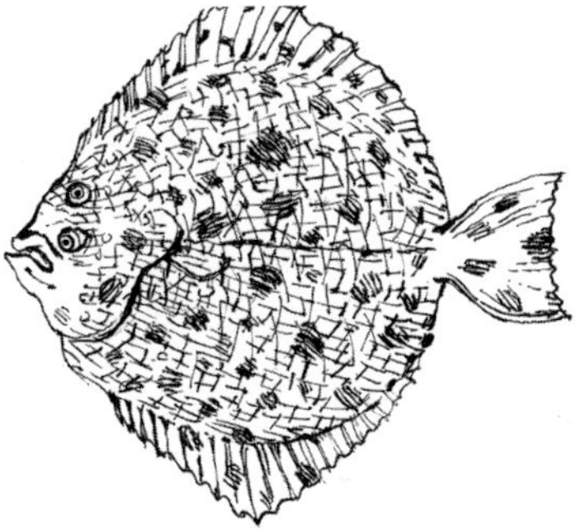

All three fish – plaice, sole and turbot – have similar characteristics and are fished for in exactly the same way. Whichever species you catch, the method used never varies. With the exception of St Ouen's Bay, the fisherman will expect to find he has caught a plaice, but at St Ouen's he will have no idea what he has caught until the fish is bagged.

As far as spiking is concerned, there is a slightly different technique required between spiking with an agricultural fork and a specially made spike. Quite simply a fork does not have barbs and so there is nothing to stop the fish from just falling off the prongs. It is necessary to be bit more patient when fishing with a fork – the prod into the sand must be positive and, if contact is made, you must be able to react very quickly by not withdrawing the fork from the sand until a hand has been placed underneath the catch to ensure that you do not lose it. When fishing with a specially made barbed spike this is not a matter of concern, the fish does not slide off.

Spiking is a bit of a guessing game. You thrust your chosen tool, spike or fork into the sand in the belief, or hope, that you will drive it into the back of a flat fish that is hiding just below the surface. For the uninitiated the idea of trying to find the spot in St Ouen's Bay, or the vast expanse of sand that is uncovered by the receding tide at La Rocque, that a plaice has decided to have a little rest might seem rather far-fetched. However, as with all types of fishing, one quickly learns where the best areas are. You recall places where you have been successful in the past, the type of sand from which you caught your fish, the areas of weed that give some protection, gullies which the fish use as they go down with the falling tide, and innumerable pointers and guides. It is believed that if you disturb a flat fish it will return to roughly the same area, having swum a triangular route. So the disappointment of treading on that large fish which has got away is tempered by the thought that if you wait a while it may return.

Flat fish do not make it easy for the low water fisherman. Their colouring renders it difficult to spot them. If they are completely buried you may see their outline in the sand and occasionally they leave their eyes poking out above the surface. The most common *modus operendi* is to have a spike in each hand and pump them into the sand as you walk along, rather in the fashion of a cross-country skier.

If using nets it is necessary to ensure that the net stays as close to the seabed as possible ensuring that nothing escapes beneath. Remember that these are bottom fish which are not very thick and which can slip through a gap of 5 centimetres or so. As with spiking, catching flatfish in nets is very much a guessing game but if you guess right it can be rewarding.

Having used the word 'slip' in the previous paragraph, the tale is told of a young lady – she was a girl de Ste Croix – who when walking her dogs along the tide line saw a shape in the sand which she instantly recognised as a plaice. Having none of the usual means of catching the fish and taking it home, she improvised by removing her slip, gathered the plaice up in it, and proudly took her catch home neatly wrapped in her petticoat.

There are many ways of cooking flatfish, be they plaice, sole or turbot, but before the advent of modern trendy cooking, our catch would normally have been fried, in butter, and eaten with boiled potatoes and possibly a vegetable.

8 TROTS, POTS and NETS

Trots Lines

Leaving a line of baited hooks on the beach, just above low water mark, or higher, is a well established form of fishing and there are two principal ways of doing this. The first method requires that the ends of a rope be firmly attached, either by tying them to rocks, or by using an anchor or two, so that the rope stretches across a gully. Onto this rope, usually weighted down with stones, a number of lines with baited hooks are attached. Then the fisherman goes back on the next tide to collect his catch. In selecting the gully or gullies used it is hoped that these are routes used by fish either making their way up with the rising tide or going back to deeper water on the falling tide.

Obviously care must be taken not to leave hooks where children or animals can get themselves caught. If you come across a line of stones in amongst the rocks it is probably where a trot has been set at some time.

The other method of setting trots is by attaching a line with a baited hook to a peg, a bit like an old-fashioned tent peg, and staking out an area of beach where you hope to be successful. Attach one baited line to each peg and the pegs not necessarily in a straight row. Again you must be aware of the hazards you are leaving behind.

The trots are set to catch fish but they do not discriminate between fish and anything else that might come along. It is always possible that you might find a sea bird caught up and drowned on a trot. As a direct result of such an occurrence I know of one man who, having found a dead bird on his trot, was sufficiently distressed that he never set trots again.

I have never been an enthusiast of setting trots and on the few occasions I have tried it my success rate was badly affected by seagulls which, upon seeing a captive meal in a couple of feet of water, were frenziedly feeding upon my catch before I was able to collect it. The simple solution to this problem is of course to lay trots by day and collect the catch after dark.

Set Nets

This is similar to laying a trot line but here the gap between the rocks is spanned by a net. It must be borne in mind that the net has to be firmly weighted at the base to stop anything swimming underneath and have floats on the top edge to give maximum catchment area. A set net needs to be checked every time the tide goes out, as you cannot leave a net full of fish stranded on a dry beach. However, not having access to a net, this is something I have never tried.

Towards the end of the German Occupation the occupying forces built a number of fish traps on island beaches in the hope that they could increase their supply of fish. One scheme involved positioning upright poles on Grève d'Azette beach to which wire netting and the tennis nets from the nearby courts were attached in the hope that fish would be trapped on the outgoing tide. One such contraption was positioned about four hundred metres from La Grande Charrière slipway. There are people who remember this trap but so far I have been unable to find anyone who can recall ever seeing anything worthwhile being caught. There is, however, a reference in Leslie Sinel's *Occupation Diary* of a good catch being taken during March 1945 in similar traps in St Brelade's Bay.

Pots and Traps

Whilst it is more common for lobster pots, or crab pots, to be dropped in strings into deep water it is possible to set a single pot in a pool in amongst the rocks. The pool has to be deep enough to keep the pot covered and anyone leaving such a pot would need to check it over fairly regularly although not necessarily every tide. Again something I have not done.

I occasionally went rod and line fishing from the pier at Ronez Quarry with Jim Le Couteur's father and he told me a tale about one of the crane drivers who, at the end of the day, would lower a pot onto the sea bed. It was left overnight and in the morning it was craned back up. He added that the crane driver was usually well rewarded for his trouble.

9 WHAT TO DO WITH OLD SHELLS

The use of crushed shells in the fowl house has already been mentioned in the sections dealing with limpets and winkles, but this was not the only use to which discarded shells were put.

They were used for decorative purposes. There are many properties in Jersey which still have shells embedded into gate pillars and gable ends, as well as in their gardens. Of the local shells, ormer and scallop were particular favourites, with cockles, limpets and winkles also playing a minor role in the finished work. Local shells were supplemented by shells brought back from overseas. In the mid to late nineteenth century Jersey had a flourishing mercantile marine and seamen returning from long-distance voyages would bring home souvenirs, including exotic shells. It is still possible to see conch shells on top of gate pillars, many of which will have been there for well over a hundred years.

The shell gardens on Le Mont Les Vaux are a modern tourist attraction. Originally the hobby of a previous owner, they have been commercialised and now attract thousands of visitors each year. With the exception of some scallop shells and some ormer shells very few of the shells used here will have passed through the hands of a low water fisherman.

Whilst on the way down to low water, or on the way back, numbers of pretty coloured shells would have been collected, especially by children. Some of these ended up being transformed into little crinoline ladies. A few limpet shells for the dress, half a cockle shell for the hat, winkles for the face and puff sleeves, the whole given a lick of paint and tourists bought them as souvenirs to take home. Similarly it was possible to make various animals and birds. Shells were also used for decorating small boxes, lamps and innumerable other items and in the making of necklaces and bracelets – souvenir items which might attract a tourist's eye. Not strictly a by-product of low water fishing but certainly a use for discarded shells, and one must not forget the ormer shell, with three winkle feet, that served as an ashtray.

Discarded ormer shells with circular holes cut into them suggest that once the ormers had been eaten some of the empty shells proved to be a cheap source of raw material for button makers. With their mother of pearl lining they made very pretty buttons.

I must admit to having been surprised to find a couple of references, from the mid-nineteenth century, to the export of ormer shells to Birmingham, where they were used in the city's papier maché industry.

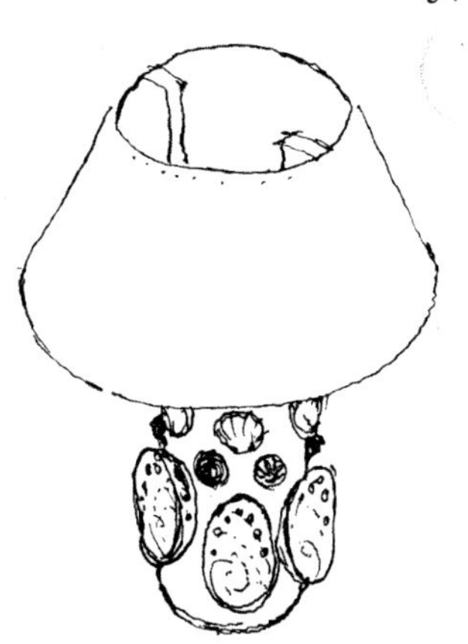

My wife's grandmother was very good at crochet work and amongst the range of items she produced was a milk jug cover. Always with yellow winkle shells weighing down the pointed edges to ensure that flies were prevented from getting into the jug. They were delicate little crocheted pieces, invariably with a milk jug pattern in the centre.

Although I would have been surprised to find a live scallop at low water, it is not uncommon to find empty scallop shells on the beach or on the rocks and farmers had a use for the rounded half of them. In the days when cows were milked by hand, the milk was directed into the milking can through a muslin cloth which was stretched loosely across the opening of the can and which was very often weighted down by a scallop shell. The milk jet was directed into the shell from where it overflowed and gently filtered down through the muslin, minus any bits of straw and other detritus, into the waiting can.

The flat side of a scallop shell makes an ideal scraper and rod and line fishermen use them to remove the scales from bass and other scaly fish.

Shells served one more serious purpose in the lives of our forebears. The island has no natural resource from which lime could be produced. Lime mortar for the construction of the castles was imported, from France or from England, but there was nothing left over for building homes. At the start of the nineteenth century a number of lime kilns were built in Jersey, and lime was produced by burning seashells. This lime had a number of uses in the building industry as well as being used by farmers as a soil conditioner on their land. At that time the Gorey oyster fisheries were getting under way and supplied some shells, but not sufficient to meet demand. The limited local supply was augmented by cargoes of shells brought home, as ballast, in ships engaged in taking surplus apples from Jersey to the cider manufacturers of Somerset.

10 SEAWEED – VRAIC – WRACK

To include a section on seaweed might seem to be stretching the subject to extremes, but there is one seaweed which islanders have collected regularly for the table. Although it is unlikely that it is still collected today, carrageen moss was on the menu for many years. It made something of a comeback during the German Occupation, when any variation to the somewhat meagre diet was welcomed. Opinions as to what it tasted like vary. In her book, *Jersey Occupation Diary*, Nan Le Ruez makes reference to collecting carrageen moss at La Pulente, and tells of making a blancmange type dessert with the addition of potato flour. She must have liked it because she also notes taking a carrageen moss pudding when visiting. On the other hand Frank Keiller, in his book *Prison Without Bars*, describes it as a disgusting jelly which tasted of iodine. My personal recollection is of eating it as a substitute custard, or blancmange, and I seem to recall looking forward to it being served.

During the Occupation carrageen moss was not only eaten but, in various forms, it was used in a number of different ways particularly by pharmacists and one local hairdresser was known to have used it as a setting lotion.

Some seaweeds, that is to say a number of different species, are edible and people still go down to the rocks to collect it for the table. I am not aware of this still being done in Jersey but it is certainly not unknown in Ireland.

Within the Island, the best known use of seaweed is as a fertilizer, and it has been used on the land since time immemorial. In season, farmers would go down and collect it by the cart load to spread on the land, scenes immortalized by Edmund Blampied prints. At the end of their day's fishing, before heading back up the beach, many low water fishermen would cover their catch by filling their basket with seaweed. My father in law regularly filled his basket in this way and when he got home, unless a piece was hung outside the back door as a weather forecasting aid, the seaweed would either be spread on the garden, or put on the compost heap. Previous generations would have also collected it as fuel for the fire.

There are many benefits derived from seaweed and one commercial activity, which flourished some years ago on the island of Lihou, just off the west coast of Guernsey, was the production of iodine.

In the late nineteenth century a fashionable way of raising money for good causes was to collect various types of seaweeds and stick them into books which were then sold at church bazaars and similar places. A number of these books still exist but their value, particularly to marine biologists, is unfortunately very limited, as the collectors rarely, if ever, noted from where they had collected the seaweeds they used.

If the pickings have been disappointing and the low water fisherman is feeling a bit disappointed with his catch, he can always reflect upon the natural beauty of his surroundings. The colours and shapes of the innumerable seaweeds are very pleasing to the eye, particularly when under water and, for people who have never ventured amongst the rocks, a wander down the beach, particularly to those rocks a bit further out, could be a very therapeutic experience.

11 COLLECTING BAIT

Can going down the beach to collect bait be classified as low water fishing? In this book it is. Depending on what they are trying to catch, small crabs, sandeels, limpets, shrimps, prawns, razor fish and various worms are all used as bait by rod and line fishermen and many of them are also used for baiting pots.

I have already dealt with catching lady crabs and green crabs, but there are other tiny crabs which make good bait and rod and line men will set traps for them. A length of plastic guttering left on the rock makes an ideal shelter for small moulting crabs to hide under and by lifting the guttering the bait hunter has all the small crabs he requires in one place with no great effort required to retrieve them. An old car tyre will also attract these tiny crabs whose claws are not a problem.

We know how to collect sandeels, limpets, shrimps, prawns, razorfish and so on, which just leaves us with the worms.

There are three basic worms. The lugworm, which is dug out from the beach or from a dried out harbour bed. It is a large, reddish-brown, sluggish and rather soft-bodied worm which is not too difficult to collect. A garden fork, some knowledge of what you are looking for, and a tin to put them in is all that is required. They live about twenty centimetres under the surface and by turning over the sand they are exposed.

The second worm is the 'white cat'. It has a whitish stripe and is collected in exactly the same way as the lug worm. It does however require more effort to collect, as there are not so many of them, and they move a lot faster. They are smaller than the lug worm, six or seven centimetres, and resemble a centipede. That is to say they have numerous legs.

The third worm is a close relative. The 'red cat' has a reddish stripe and is found amongst the rocks by moving the stones behind which they shelter. Both the 'red cat' and the 'white cat' are much firmer than the lug worm and are less likely to fall off the hook. Red cat will nip you if you are not careful.

The beach just below Castle Street was a favourite place for digging bait until it was swallowed up by land reclamation, and St Aubin and Gorey harbours have been forked over many times by people looking to collect a few worms.

It is not unknown for rod and line men to prepare a favourite fishing spot by feeding it beforehand with chervie. (There was an *Evening Post* fishing columnist who wrote under the name 'Chervie' for many years, and I have used his spelling). Chervie was considered essential if the target was the grey mullet and was simply a mix of any small marine life which you cared to go and collect, including crabs and sandeel, especially very small sandeels.

Preparation was not difficult. All that was required was to put the 'ingredients' through a fine mincer. It was stored in jars and used as required, but it did sometimes smell a bit strong. I recall making chervie, with my friend Jim Le Couteur, when we mashed up green crabs and put them in an old paint tin, the lid of which we pressed very firmly back on. We then buried the tin in the sand, about one hundred yards from where I now live, and although we took cross references we were never able to find it again. Maybe it is still there.

In theory, a spoonful or two of chervie would be thrown into the sea for a few days prior to the day planned to do some serious fishing and the fish would all congregate at that spot and be queuing up to be caught. It did not always go according to plan.

12 PRESERVING

The arrival of refrigeration and the fact that most homes now have a refrigerator, with deep freezing facilities, has made most others forms of preserving foodstuffs, at home, redundant. It should none the less be recalled that various forms of marine life lend themselves to preserving and that one or more of the main food preserving techniques – drying, salting, pickling, smoking and bottling – were once an important part of household management in the island and that fish, including species caught by low water fishermen, would have been included in that process.

Drying

There are areas around the coast of Jersey the nomenclature of which suggest that fish was dried on a commercial scale and it therefore follows that the ability to dry fish, surplus to immediate requirement, was well within the ability of Jerseymen. The local Courts were being asked to adjudicate in disputes about the conger fisheries before 1204, and evidence of dried conger was found in the stores of Henry VIII's flagship *Mary Rose* when it was recovered. As previously mentioned, as late as the 1970s my brothers and I would dry sandeels. Octopus, before they all went away, were also easy to dry, and to keep. No great skill was required for drying, just sunshine.

Salting

In view of the Island's involvement in the Newfoundland fisheries there can be no doubt that Jerseymen knew how to salt fish. Even today there still exist a considerable number of large granite salting troughs in Jersey. Although many of these would have been used for salting down a pig or two, rather than fish, the principle is the same. Not all salting was done in these heavy troughs for there were also pottery jars and wooden tubs for salting and with ample supplies of salt it would have been a simple job to salt down any fish, surplus to current need, for later in the year.

Pickling

I have no direct experience of fish or crustaceans being pickled, although I have seen references to limpets being pickled. As there were large scale enterprises pickling cockles and mussels in the UK, it would seem probable that it also happened in Jersey.

Smoking

Postcards depicting old Jersey kitchens invariably show an elderly couple sitting in front of a large open fireplace, sometimes with hams and various other items hanging within the confines of the hearth. It is not always easy to identify what exactly is hanging up there, but included are items which may well have been fish. Although I have been unable to confirm that fish collected from the low water mark were preserved in this way both conger and sandeel would have been comparatively simple to smoke.

Bottling

The bottling of fruit and vegetables was a regular activity in many Jersey households. I well recall jars of fruit, pears and plums and the like, and also various vegetables stored in sealed jars in the larders of relatives. Suitable fish were also bottled and it came as no surprise to learn from a Jerseyman who, when living in England, received the occasional kilner jar full of ormers, cooked and ready to eat. He usually re-heated them in a casserole before eating them, with mashed potatoes and gravy, and there were always sufficient for more than one meal.

13 OCCUPATION TALES

Any references made about access to the island's beaches during the years 1940 to1945 are likely to be controversial because I have always believed that it was necessary to have a pass to go down from the foreshore, as witnessed by my father-in-law's fishing permit. However, a well respected local authority on Occupation matters has no recollection of being denied access, other than in areas of military importance.

There are a number of references in Leslie Sinel's book, *The German Occupation of Jersey: A Complete Diary*, detailing fishing regulations issued by the Germans which confirm that they did close some or all of the beaches at various times. On 5th August, 1940, an order was issued prohibiting 'all fishing and the use of the beaches'. This order was relaxed the next day. By December 1940 there were a number of military zones established which were at first fenced in but by the turn of the year the local population was warned that these areas were being mined. And so it went on. On D-Day, in June 1944, all low water fishing was suspended. This was followed by an order three days later declaring all beaches to be out of bounds, an order which was marginally relaxed three days later when farmers were permitted, at their own risk, to go and collect *vraic*.

Certain areas were permanently out of bounds. By the end of 1941 listed beaches and certain areas of foreshore, which had been heavily mined, were declared off limits but there were still stretches of coastline to which access seems to have been permitted according to the strategic requirements of the day. On occasions the collection of the *vraic* harvest was disrupted by these closure orders and the building of concrete barriers across various slipways did not endear the Germans to the farming community.

In the Introduction I wrote that it was possible to get a pass from the occupying administration which allowed islanders to go down onto the rocks. I also referred to having to keep to the curfew and not straying into forbidden zones, but there were other considerations to be borne in mind, not least the possibility of getting hurt.

When talking to a friend who is a few years older than I am and who has known me since the Occupation years, he recalled one memorable day when he went low water fishing at L'Etacq with the Amy brothers. Although it was only target practice, and the artillery men were aiming at a target far out into St Ouen's Bay, he assured me that when the German batteries started firing their big guns it was scary and he ducked every time a shell went screaming overhead, albeit far too late to make any difference.

Not all shells exploded on impact and these, added to assorted ammunition lying about in the wrecks of ships lost during those war years, meant that many pieces of ordnance were washed up during this time. Even now, in the twenty-first century, unexploded shells are still being found. If you chance upon a rusting metal cylinder you are well advised to leave it alone and report it to the appropriate authority. About fifty years ago a mortar bomb was discovered near the bathing pool at Havre des Pas. This bomb was thought to have come from an ammunition barge which sank near the Dog's Nest rocks. In August 1957, when the bomb was found, the barge was believed to still contain much of its original cargo.

The Germans lost a number of vessels during the war as a result of which there are a variety of wrecks off the coast, many amongst the rocks along St Clement's Bay. Wandering in and around wrecks, in wartime, could be hazardous but occasionally it could be quite rewarding. Towards the end of the Occupation a group of young men, having come up from a trip down to the low water mark in St Clement's Bay, were discussing their somewhat meagre pickings when the last of the group came up with a very heavy basket. Not for him a few limpets and winkles but a basket full of coal, which he had extracted from a wreck. He went down again the next day and continued to go down on successive tides until such time as the tide made it impossible for him to reach his private little coal mine.

My father-in-law had a somewhat similar experience when he found, not coal, but a crate of brandy. Three bottles went into his basket underneath the limpets and the winkles and all well covered with seaweed as he had to pass the guard at La Rocque slip, and three into the basket of his fishing companion. They made a second trip the next day to collect the remaining six bottles. One bottle was kept, for 'medicinal purposes', his remaining five bottles he bartered.

In all wars people get killed and whereas after land battles the casualties would be taken to hospital or removed for burial, such niceties were not available to seamen and one of the hazards of low water fishing during the war years was the possibility of finding a body which had been washed up. There are still people around today who have vivid memories of making such a discovery.

As an aside, if I was aware that someone was missing at sea, whether they had been swept off a beach or fallen from a boat, even if it meant missing a big tide, I would not go low water fishing until the body had been recovered.

Living in the twenty-first century, it is difficult to truly appreciate the full extent of the shortages and of the resultant resourcefulness of the men and women who had to deal with the lack of virtually every commodity in the final months of the Occupation. A cousin told me that when he went winkling with our grandmother she would scrape up any salt crystals from dried out rock pools for use in the kitchen. She took the crystals home where they were dissolved and any debris removed, after which the solution was allowed to evaporate and the resultant salt was stored in a jar until required.

14 FLOTSAM AND JETSAM

Anyone who frequents the bays and coves of the island on a regular basis will be aware that all sorts of things get washed up, or if you are further down the beach, uncovered, by the sea.

Reports of seeing peat beds and the stumps of trees from the forests that were lost to an ever encroaching sea are undeniable evidence of considerable land loss, but the sighting of paved roads and worked stone are highly unlikely to be anything other than the remains of vraicing routes. These were tracks cut through the rocks to facilitate the collection of seaweed, and should not be considered to be the remains of farms or villages.

Over the years people have made collections of clay pipes, glass, pottery and coins which they have come across but the movement of the tides, in conjunction with the abrasive action of the sand, has damaged such items considerably and therefore they have little monetary value, unless of course they got lucky and found gold or silver.

You can never be certain what you will find when you go down with the tide and there are times when it would be surprising if you had the necessary tools with you to profit from the unexpected as evidenced by the following three stories.

Story One: In the nineteenth century there were numerous shipwrecks and debris would inevitably come ashore. After a severe storm in 1897, an item in a local newspaper reported the usual and seemingly commonplace finds of rigging, spars, planks, boxes of merchandise, casks of wines and spirits, etc. but on this occasion there was also a great number of dead bullocks. The bullock carcasses were taken to the knackers yard at Bellozanne where they were 'turned to profitable account'. The paper does not tell us exactly what they did with them.

Story Two: One can only guess at the reaction of the person who went down to the beach at St Ouen, one hundred and seventy years earlier, and found a dead whale washed up in the bay. There are two written references to this event. In one the whale is described as being about three and a half perch long (an interesting unit of measurement) and in the other it is reportedly 71 feet long. Evidence of this event can still be seen at Vinchelez de Bas Manor where, 285 years later, the jaw bones are still visible. We are told that 'they made much oil for burning' from the carcass.

Story Three: Within living memory two unusual animals were reported to be living in the Icho Tower area of St Clement's Bay. An expedition was mounted, traps were set, and one very wild mink was captured. Its companion was not caught but was not seen again.

CONCLUSION

For the most part this work is a collection of my personal reminiscences, with some historical facts and a few added tales told by friends and acquaintances, to whom I am grateful. I believe the contents of the book, written whilst on various holidays over the passed ten years or so, to be an honest and accurate account of one facet of island life in the latter half of the twentieth century.

If not totally excluded, I hope that the proverbial exaggerations of fishermen have been muted and that what is included within the covers of this book will ring true to many islanders, and hopefully not only to Jerseymen but also to other Channel Islanders, who after reading the book will reflect with affection upon a way of life which has now almost disappeared.

The influx of continental workers into Jersey, especially the Portuguese speakers and more lately the Polish nationals, has depleted the stock of some of the previously plentiful species, particularly the limpet. This has happened since I gave up serious low water fishing after damaging my leg in 1998 and I feel unable to comment on events since 2000.

And finally, I am told by a local man who married a Madeirian girl that, although it does not feature in his top ten 'must do again' culinary experiences, the occasional meal which includes raw limpet is not as daunting as would at first appear.

Chacqu'un à son gôut.

The one that got away
or
Tomorrow I'm going to Seymour